Serious Educational Games

Serious Educational Games
From Theory to Practice

Edited by
Leonard A. Annetta
North Carolina State University

Foreword by
Jerry Heneghan
Founder and CEO, Virtual Heroes Inc.
www.virtualheroes.com
President, North Carolina Advanced Learning Technology Association
www.ncalta.org
Research Triangle Park, North Carolina

SENSE PUBLISHERS
ROTTERDAM / TAIPEI

A C.I.P. record for this book is available from the Library of Congress.

ISBN 978-90-8790-379-4 (paperback)
ISBN 978-90-8790-380-0 (hardback)

Published by: Sense Publishers,
P.O. Box 21858, 3001 AW Rotterdam, The Netherlands
http://www.sensepublishers.com
Printed on acid-free paper

CONTENTS

ACKNOWLEDGEMENTS

For those who know me, it is probably not surprising that my research and this edited book is grounded in video games in education. As someone who always loved competition and collaboration, researching the power of video games in education was not a stretch for me. However, it is only right to acknowledge those around me who have not only gotten me to this point but those who continue to motivate me.

First I have to mention my beautiful and loving wife Jennifer. She has stood by me through thick and thin following my crazy path from undergraduate education to NC State University by way of the University of Missouri-St. Louis. We still shake our heads at where we have gotten so early in life. She is a very competitive person as well so I know that every hurdle I face and battle I encounter Jennifer has my back. Jennifer also gave me to two most wonderful gifts in the world: my daughter Samantha and my son Joseph. These two angels motivate me daily and their unconditional love gets me through any situation the professorial deals. Joseph in particular has become my built-in reassurance that my work is worthwhile. At five years old, he lives to play games, is completely engaged and most importantly seems to have been learning from the games in which we allow him to play. What Sesame Street did for Samantha, computer games and V-Smile are now doing for Joseph. Strangely enough I also need to recognize my dogs, Mocha and Honey. Mocha was the focus of my first storyboard for a children's video game even though it has yet to come to fruition.

I would be remised if I didn't mention my parents. Mike and Marie Annetta are the most supportive and loving parents a person could ever want. Supporting every decision I've made and pushing me to always give 100% laid the foundation for what I do today. My sister Rosemary and brother Michael were always my teachers. Their accomplishments and mistakes taught me many lessons and I can never thank them enough. My niece Gianna and my nephew Derrick deserve some credit. Derrick was actually the person who opened my eyes to multiplayer games while I was working on my doctorate. It was then that I saw the potential power of games as learning tools.

I doubt if I could have accomplished as much as I have without the love and support of my in-laws Bill and Kathy Glotzabch. Their support, especially as I went through graduate school with two babies, will never be forgotten or unappreciated. My doctoral advisor Jim Shymansky opened the door into higher education for me and wouldn't allow me to fail or quit. He still is and will always be Pappa Jim. I would also like to acknowledge Charles and Doris Matthews for their love and support through graduate school and during my time at NC State. Carl Hoagland and Phil Fraundorf, two professors at the University of Missouri-St. Louis, who encouraged me to pursue technology as a vehicle for teaching and learning science and particularly Phil for introducing me to 3D virtual environments.

Joe Rotellini, my college football coach, also needs to be recognized. While decided whether or not I should pursue a Ph.D., Coach convinced me that it would be the best decision I will ever make. He was right. John Penick, my current department head, and Dean Kay Moore of N.C. State University gave me my first job in the professorial, and supported a new faculty members crazy ideas of going after funding to research 3D virtual environments and video games. Similarly, all of my colleagues and friends who have gone down this crazy road-thank you.

I need to also acknowledge my college roommates who bought the original Nintendo that provided a platform for some serious battles between classes. The name *Lentendo* still resonates guys. Finally, I would like to acknowledge my brother-in-law Billy, who lived with us for some time after he graduated high school. The late nights playing Madden football and the ensuing fights were some of the best times I had playing video games Game on Dude!

JERRY HENEGHAN

FOREWORD

Serious Educational Games: From Theory to Practice

Long-term competitiveness requires a skilled work force. To compete in a knowledge economy, high-tech industries require proficiency in math, science, computer literacy and engineering -- 21st century equivalents of the three R's. The ability of our children to compete and prosper in the 21st century will depend on innovative new methods to accelerate education, increase proficiency and reduce training costs.

The convergence of education and gaming technologies represents an evolution of learning. Well-designed "serious games" (computer game technology used for training and education purposes) teach by stimulating the imagination, sparking curiosity, fostering discussion and encouraging a spirit of competitive exploration across a variety of domains.

The term "Serious Games" was first used as the title of a book by Clark C. Abt in 1970. The book illustrated the power of games to simulate a simplified version of reality and thus help people understand the variables, causes, and effects impacting decisions in the real world through role playing exercises. With the availability of commercial-off-the-shelf (COTS) interactive technologies, the credibility of serious games has grown steadily over the past decade.

The work of scholars such as Henry Jenkins at MIT and James Paul Gee at University of Wisconsin have shown that video game technologies offer the most promise for reaching, engaging and instructing our students. Recent reports such as the Federation of American Scientists' Summit on Educational Games Report (2006), the New Media Consortium and EDUCAUSE's 2006 and 2007 Horizon Reports have demonstrated that the use of video game technology for education is gaining momentum as an effective means to improve learning outcomes.

This book takes an unprecedented look at the evolving use of "serious games" for educational purposes along with some related advanced learning technologies such as Multi -User Virtual Environments (MUVEs), haptics and biofeedback technology. It presents a collection of chapters that portray the theoretical and research foundation for the education use of serious games from the perspective of experts in the field who also understand the practical application of serious games. The book also provides an overview of problem-based learning as an instructional approach using the immersive characteristics of modern game technology driven by engaging narratives, character development and back-story. It provides a breadth of perspectives that transition from 'what we think" to "what we know" regarding serious games and their use in education.

It is encouraging that editor Len Annetta and the authors have taken an empirical approach to the study of educational serious games – one of research and grounded theory, rather than advocacy. This book breaks new ground and is an important step in the process of moving from hype regarding serious games to a more firm foundation in the study of serious games in education. Through this important book, Annetta shows us how we can take advantage of game technologies in order to transform education in an increasingly outdated educational system. Written in a clear, lucid and direct manner, Dr. Len Annetta makes the central themes of this book easily accessible to professional as well as lay readers. It will benefit educators, school administrators, policy makers, cognitive researchers, content developers and parents regarding contemporary theory, design and use of serious games for education.

Before embarking on the exploration of this book a few definitions might be helpful:

- *STEM:* educational initiative focused on the domains of science, technology, engineering and mathematics

- *Simulation*: a representation of real life that accurately demonstrates a physical or simulated process or phenomenon

- *Games*: deliberately simplified representations of phenomenon based on goal-directed and competitive activities conducted within a framework of established rules

- *Serious Games:* Game technology used for other than purely entertainment purposes such as strategic messaging, training and education and mission planning and rehearsal. Serious games operate at the nexus of where gaming and computer graphics technology meet with instructional design and the needs of modeling and simulation.

- *Multi -User Virtual Environments (MUVEs:* MUVEs enable multiple simultaneous participants to:
  - access virtual architectures configured for learning
  - to interact with digital artifacts
  - represent themselves through graphical "avatars,"
  - communicate both with other participants and with computer-based agents
  - enact collaborative activities of various types.

- *Virtual Worlds* A virtual world is a computer-based simulated environment intended for its users to inhabit and interact via avatars. This habitation usually is represented in the form of two or three-dimensional graphical representations of humanoids (or other graphical or text-based avatars). Some, but not all, virtual worlds allow for multiple users.

Enjoy!

Jerry Heneghan
Founder and CEO, Virtual Heroes Inc.
www.virtualheroes.com
President, North Carolina Advanced Learning Technology Association
www.ncalta.org
Research Triangle Park, North Carolina
October 2007

REFERENCES

Federation of American Scientists' Summit on Educational Games Report (2006)
http://www.fas.org/gamesummit/

EDUCAUSE's 2006 Horizon Report (2006)
http://www.nmc.org/pdf/2006HorizonReport.pdf

New Media Consortium
http://www.nmc.org/pdf/2007HorizonReport.pdf

LEONARD A. ANNETTA & MENG-TZU CHENG

CHAPTER 1

Why Educational Video Games?

We don't stop playing because we grow old, we grow old because we stop playing~ Oliver Wendell Holmes

INTRODUCTION

A 2005 report by the Business Roundtable entitled Tapping America's Potential: The Education for Innovation Initiative expressed "deep concern about the United States' ability to sustain its scientific and technological superiority through this decade and beyond" (p. 1). The report called for a sense of urgency and for immediate action to secure a prosperous future for our country and our children. How can this monumental task be accomplished? How can we reach children who have been called the *Net Generation* and *Digital Natives*? One potential explanation could be through Serious Educational Games. In 2003, the Serious Games movement was started as an approach to empower people with video game technology in teaching and training. This chapter provides brief explanations for the questions: 1) Why use educational video games?, 2) What are 21st Century skills?, 3) What is play and should it be in schools? and how educational games are being used at North Carolina State University.

WHY USE EDUCATIONAL GAMES?

Video game industry today approaches yearly revenues of $15 billion and approximately 3.38 billion hours of game play. The game playing population falls between the ages of 10 - 34 with the majority of the population between 14-19. Games are not just played, they are talked about, read about, ''cheated'', fantasized about, altered, become models for every day life, and for the formation of subjectivity and intersubjectivity. There is a politics, an economy, a history, social structure and function, and an everyday lived-experience of the game (de Castell, 2003). Craft (2004) believes the method of instruction embodied in video games has potential for non-self-referential disciplines, particularly science.

The Federation of American Scientists called video games the next great discovery, as they offer a way to captivate students to the point that they will spend hours learning on their own time. Their report stated that educational video games are not an investment that private industry is capable of taking. There is a need for the federal government to drive the movement forward with both financial and political support (Federation of American Scientists, 2006). *Immune Attack* (http://www.fas.org/immuneattack), *Food Force* (http://www.food-force.com), *Discover Babylon* (http://www.discoverbabylon.org), and *Quest Atlantis* (http://atlantis.crlt.indiana.edu/start/index.html) are examples of games developed as a result of this drive that can be used for educational purposes.

These educational games commonly require the use of logic, memory, problem-solving, critical thinking skills, visualization, and discovery. Moreover, the use of these gaming technologies requires that users manipulate virtual objects using electronic tools and develop an understanding of the complex systems being modeled.

Generally speaking, these educational games seem to be effective in enhancing motivation and increasing student interest in subject matter, yet the extent to which this translates into more effective learning is less clear. The lack of empirical data, due primarily to the scarcity of systematic investigations into the cognitive impact of serious games, forces us to turn to prior work investigating the impact of interactive computer simulations for hard evidence.

Educators and scientists repeatedly return to the conclusion that one advantage of educational games is that games tend to generate a much higher level of students' positive emotional engagement, thus making the learning experience more motivating and appealing (Rieber et al., 1998), improving participation and achievement (Jayakanthan, 2002). Video games motivate learning by challenging, providing curiosity, beauty, fantasy, fun, and social recognition. They reach learners and passive students who don't do well in conventional settings (Tanner & Jones, 2000; Dede, 2004). By representing the simulations through gaming conventions, educators can potentially increase engagement while fostering deeper learning, as learners engage in critical and recursive game play, whereby they generate hypotheses about the game, develop plans and strategies, observe their results, and readjust their hypotheses (Gee, 2003b).

Stealth learning, coined by Douglas Crockford in 1987, is designed at making a fun game with no overt teaching involved but to have the enjoyment enhanced as you learn more about the subject matter (Falstein, 2005). It can be argued that learning takes place best in story-based, human-centered circumstances (Cognition and Technology Group at Vanderbilt, 1993).

Designing human-centered educational games that have rich storylines is not a magic bullet nor is it an easy undertaking. The implications for designing educational games include blended motivation and self-regulated learning (Rieber et al., 1998). Today's gamers learn differently within the context of virtual worlds. Gee (2003a) stated the practice of learning a video game is an enculturation practice that involves not only learning the mechanics of game play, but learning how to negotiate the context of play, the terms and practices of a game's players, and the design choices of its developers. These levels of engagement are what Gee calls internal and external design grammars for a given domain. These design grammars are consistent in any competitive or collaborative play environment.

A player learns to think critically about the simulation while at the same time gaining embedded knowledge through interacting with the environment. Games provide learners the opportunity to learn by doing, experience situations first-hand, and role-play. This establishes the proliferation of gaming in today's learners (Rickard & Oblinger, 2004). Virtual learning environments allow for development of higher levels of learning and collaboration skills (Gibbs, 1999), and improved practical reasoning skills (Wood & Stewart, 1987).

WHAT ARE 21ST CENTURY SKILLS?

If we are to reach tomorrow's leaders today, it is crucial we design curricula around the foreseen skills needed to be successful in the 21st Century (see chapter 2 of this book for clear examples of 21st Century skills). Income and wealth in the 21st century will come from applying technology and new ideas to create new products and processes. Adding value to products and processes is the key to growing jobs and income in this new economic environment (Aubert, 2004). Why is this so important? Jobs once located in the United States are now being outsourced or off-shored. The National Committee on Science, Engineering and Public Policy (2006) reported some alarming statistics:

- For the cost of one engineer in the United States, a company can hire eleven in India.
- 38% of the scientists and engineers in America holding doctorates were born abroad.
- Chemical companies closed seventy facilities in the U.S. in 2004. Of 120 new chemical plants being built around the world with price tags of $1 billion or more, one is in the U.S. while fifty are in China.
- In 1997 China had fewer than fifty research centers managed by multinational corporations. By 2004 China held over six hundred.
- For the first time, the most capable high-energy particle accelerator on earth will reside outside the United States.
- In a recent international test involving mathematical understanding, U.S. students finished in 27th place among participating nations.
- About two-thirds of the students studying chemistry and physics in U.S. high schools are taught by teachers with no major or certificate in the subject. In the case of math taught in grades 5-12, the fraction is one-half.
- In one recent period, low-wage employers like Wal-Mart (now the nation's largest employer) and McDonald's created 44% of all new jobs. High-wage employers created only 29%.
- In 2003 foreign students earned 59% of the engineering doctorates awarded in U.S. universities.
- In 2003 only three American companies ranked among the top ten recipients of patents granted by the U.S. Patent Office.

- In Germany, 36% of undergraduates receive their degrees in science and engineering. In China, the corresponding figure is 59%, and in Japan it is 66%. In the U.S., the share is 32%. In the case of engineering, the U.S. share is 5%, as compared with 50% in China.

The workers of the 21st century must have science and mathematics skills, creativity, information and communication technologies (ICT) skills, and the ability to solve complex problems (Business-Higher Education Forum, 2005). The transformation of learning in many other countries provides models to consider how linking education and the economy benefits students, businesses, and society (Kozma & Voogt, 2003). The use of sophisticated information technologies in every aspect of education has the potential to provide a powerful lever for this transformation (Jones, 2003). The United States is not developing its workforce with skills in expert thinking and complex communications to meet the needs of the 21st century, global, knowledge-based economy (Levy & Murnane, 2004).

WHAT IS PLAY AND SHOULD IT BE IN SCHOOLS?

The idea of playing to learn is not a new concept. Sociologists and anthropologists have tended to treat play as a human activity in which they analyze the principal characteristics observed in the age of the player (Caillois, 1961). This stems from Groos's theory (1898) of pre-exercise, which led him to affirm that we do not play because we are young, but we have a youth because we must play to practice. Play systematically confronts the child with a learning situation that could only be located within his/her area of close development. That is, it would involve a task located slightly above the acquired skills (Vygotsky, 1967).

Childhood is a time for constructing the relationship between the world implied by play, the decision, the initiative of the player who organizes the activity, the rule, whatever its origin, the absence of consequences (gratuity or futility), and the uncertainty of the results (Brougere, 1999). Learning to play is learning to master situations marked by the second degree, the necessary metacommunication (Bateson, 1973). We must relearn to pretend—learn that things are not as they seem but within the context of a controlled and negotiated action between players. This is most noticeable in the disconnect between role play and game from child to adult (Bruner, 1983). These lines are becoming blurry, as more adults are engaging in video games.

Rieber, Smith, and Noah (1998) argue that digital games engage players in productive play, which gives reason for renewed optimism for using games to support learning in leveraging the increasing power of the computer to immerse the player in interactive simulated worlds. Games allow the player to increasingly better understand the logic behind rules and express themselves as individuals through the roles they portray within a game. If we are able to successfully participate in video games and simulation, it is because as children we learned to master rules through play (Corbeil, 1999).

Clegg (1991) argued that the instructional context that envelops gaming is a more important predictor of learning than the game itself. Specifically, how the game is contextualized, the kinds of cooperative and collaborative learning activities embedded in game play, and the quality and nature of debriefing are all critically important elements of the gaming experience. Engaging simulations provide an environment for the cycling of assimilation and accommodation which is referred to as cognitive disequilibrium and resolution. Simulations succeed as teaching tools when they initiate cognitive disequilibrium and resolution while allowing the player to be successful (Piaget, 1975).

PRACTICE (HOW)

The power of video game technology can be embraced in many ways. Two such applications will be described. The first use of video games is as a platform for distance learning. The second application is as an instrument for teaching and learning course material.

The Wolf Den

At North Carolina State University's College of Education, a virtual world was created as a platform for distance learning and video game creation for practicing teachers. The *Wolf Den*, as it is called, is a virtual leaning environment where synchronous, online courses are taught and where students engage in the design and creation of role-play games. Specifically, a course entitled Introduction to 3D Multiuser Online Role-Play Games[1], introduces inservice science teachers to the game creation process.

Using much of the aforementioned theory as a framework for the construction of this course, the *Wolf Den* originally set out to find a way to deliver online learning synchronously and to investigate if practicing teachers could create their own role play science games.

As high-speed connectivity becomes more pervasive and service converge increases, students enrolled in distance courses desire synchronous interaction without leaving the comfort of their home. This makes sense since we have been programmed through the preK-12 schooling to interact with our peers and teachers in real time. *Wolf Den* not only provided a quality distance-learning platform, but also through the inclusion of a Voice over Internet Protocol (VoIP) solution, real-time conversations were exchanged while both the instructor and student were visually captivated in the 3D world. Moreover, students enrolled and taught in the *Wolf Den* are exposed to immersive artifacts that can be manipulated as easy as, or sometimes easier then, in the real world.

An example mini game created in the *Wolf Den* allows students enrolled in the distance course to enter the laboratory and test water samples through microscopes and use the chemicals they would have used in the traditional setting (Figure 1). This not only is a safe way of performing potentially dangerous science activities

5

but also begins to answer the question of how science can be delivered from a distance while giving the students authentic laboratory experiences.

Figure 1. Laboratory in the Wolf Den virtual world at NC State University

The students exposed to *Wolf Den* had very positive attitudes toward the delivery method and the interactions within the virtual learning environment (Annetta, Murray, Gull-Laird, Bohr, & Park, 2006). In addition, students with high overall perceptions of social presence scored high in terms of perceived learning and perceived satisfaction with the instructor.

Annetta and Holmes (2006) reported that using avatars, digital representations of oneself, increased social presence and built a stronger community of practice. Students who had a choice of which avatar they would like to be, reported greater course satisfaction and felt closer to their classmates and instructor than students who only could choose a male or a female avatar (Figure 2). Those students with choices could be unique, giving them a sense of individuality. Deindividuation is a state in which people lose their individuality because group members do not feel they stand out as individuals and/or individuals act if they are submerged in the group (Festinger, Pepitone, & Newcomb, 1952). This is a major detraction in online learning as it has been delivered most recently through asynchronous course management tools.

Figure 2. Avatars representing students in the Wolf Den.

The second question asked whether or not teachers could learn to design video games as a teaching and learning tool. Not only were teachers able to learn the game design and creation process, but they successfully constructed games that engaged students, built a community of peers, and helped students learn difficult science content (Annetta et al., 2006). This ability and success was a springboard to the *HI FIVES* project.

HI FIVES (Highly Interactive Fun Internet Virtual Environments in Science)[2]

HI FIVES is a joint effort of researchers in science, distance education, and computer science who are partnering with the Kenan Fellows Program (An elite teacher group) to harness the untapped potential of inexpensive, online multiuser video games to improve the IT skills and science achievement of students in grades 5 - 9. Fifteen teacher leaders and 60 participants (including seven guidance counselors) are learning how to use this technology to increase student science and math achievement and motivate their students to enter STEM-related careers. Moreover, over 200 students will learn the games design process and work closely with teachers to add the fun element to the content rich games the teachers create.

Much of the literature describes the potential of games or how off-the-shelf software can be used in the classroom (Gee, 2003a; 2003b; Prensky, 2001; Squire, 2001). *HI FIVES* is unique in the sense that it is providing a tool for teachers so they may create video games for their individual classes. Further, students will learn the game design and creation process so they can construct video games as a form of performance assessment. Through a drag-and-drop Graphical User Interface (GUI) wrapped around the Half-Life2™ game engine, participants in *HI FIVES* are creating immersive, multiuser games without knowledge of 3D art or computer programming. The development software, called *Virtuoso*, will be made

7

available to the public in October 2007 and can be ascertained from the project website[3].

All of the attributes garnered from the *Wolf Den* are being incorporated into *HI FIVES*. The idea of community of practice and social presence are at the forefront of the research being conducted. Active learning through the immersion of games is showing positive impact on the digital natives participating in the project. As opposed to watching videos, students are actively, not passively, learning content. Further, through an integrated database, teachers are able to ascertain real-time data from student decisions in the game they created.

A game create by a teacher, titled *Invicta The Invader*, was designed to teach six grade students about invasive species; specifically the red fire ant in this case. During the first phase of development, the teacher created a robust story about how fire ants made their way in the United States (figure 3). The game was merely a passive walk through of the invasion from the perspective of a fire ant. When the students took the role of developer, the obtained the vision of the teacher, researched the history of the fire ant invasion, and created a more engaging, fun educational virtual environment (figure 4).

Figure 3: The game start of Invicta The Invader

Figure 4: A screen shot of student development of Invicta The Invader depicting fire ant feeding on turtle eggs.

Video games in the classroom are not a replacement for good teaching. They are merely a supplement that engages students in the content and provides an avenue for them to learn difficult concepts of the real world in an environment in which they are accustomed.

CONCLUSION

There is still much to be done in this arena. If this is the present of how video games are being used in education, then what is the future? There is much to be done in this area and what follows is an outline of potential future research on video game technology as it pertains to education. The remainder of this text will provide you with a theoretical framework and concrete examples from which to begin your quest for answers on educational video games.

REFERENCES

Annetta, L.A., Murray, M., Gull-Laird, S., Bohr, S., & Park, J. C. (2006). Serious games: Incorporating video games in the classroom. *Educause Quarterly, 29*(3), http://www.educause.edu/apps/eq/eqm06/eqm0633.asp

Annetta, L.A., & Holmes, S. (2006) Creating presence and community in a synchronous virtual learning environment using avatars. *International Journal of Instructional Technology and Distance Learning, 3*(8), http://www.itdl.org/Journal/Aug_06/article03.htm

Aubert, J., & Reiffers, J. (2004). *Knowledge economies in the Middle East and North Africa: Toward new development strategies.* Washington, D.C.: World Bank.

Bateson, G. (1973). A theory of play and fantasy. In A.L. Herts, *Steps of an ecology of mind:* Paladin.

Brougere, G. (1999). Some elements relating to children's play and adult simulation/gaming. *Simulation & Gaming, 30*(2), 134-146.

Bruner, J. S. (1983). *Child's talk: Learning to use language.* Oxford, UK: Oxford University Press.

Business-Higher Education Forum (2005). A commitment to America's future: Responding to the crisis in mathematics & science education. Retrieved July 19, 2006, http://www.itic.org/archives/TAP %20Statement.pdf

Business Roundtable (2005). Tapping America's potential: The education for innovation initiative. Retrieved July 15, 2006, from http://www.itic.org/archives/TAP%20Statement.pdf

Caillois, R. (1961). *Man, play, and games.* New York: Free Press.

Clegg, A. A. (1991). Games and simulations in social studies education. In J. P. Shaver (ed.), *Handbook of research on social studies teaching and learning* (Vol. 523-528). New York: Macmillan. . (pp. 523-528)

Cognition and Technology Group at Vanderbilt (1993). Designing learning environments that support thinking: The Jasper series as a case study. In T. M. Duffy, Lowyck, J., & D.H. Jonassen (eds.), *Design Environments for constructivist learning.* New York: Springer-Verlag. (pp. 231-315).

Corbeil, P. (1999). Learning from children: Practical and theoretical reflections on playing and learning. *Simulation & Gaming, 30*(2), 163-180.

Craft, J. (2004). A Review of What Video Games Have to Teach Us about Learning and Literacy. *Currents in Electronic Literacy, 8.* http://www.cwrl.utexas.edu/currents/fall04/craft.html

de Castell, S., & Jenson, J. (2003). Serious play. *Journal of Curriculum Studies, 35*(6), 649-665.

Dede, C. (2004). *Distributed-learning communities as a model for educating teachers.* Paper presented at the Society of Information Technology for Teacher Educators (SITE), Atlanta, GA.

Falstein, N. (2005). Interactive stealth learning. Retrieved March 6, 2007, from http://ecolloq.gsfc.nasa.gov/archive/2002-Spring/announce.falstein.html

Federation of American Scientists. (2006). *Summit on educational games: Harnessing the power of video games for learning.* Washington, DC.

Festinger, L., Pepitone, A., & Newcomb, T. (1952). Some consequences of deindividuation in a group. *Journal of Abnormal and Social Psychology, 47,* 382-389.

Garris, R., Ahlers, R., & Driskell, J.E. (2002). Games, motivation, and learning: A research and practice model. *Simulation & Gaming, 33*(4), 441-467.

Gee, J. P. (2003a). Video games in the classroom? Retrieved February 10, 2004, *The Chronicle of Higher Education* August 15, 2003.

Gee, J. P. (2003b). *What video games have to teach us about learning.* New York: Palgrave.

Gibbs, G. R. (1999). Learning how to learn using a virtual learning environment for philosophy. *Journal of Computer Assisted Learning, 15,* 221-231.

Groos, K. (1898). *The play of animals.* New York. D. Appleton.

Jayakanthan, R. (2002). Application of computer games in the field of education. *The Electronic Library, 20*(2), 98-102.

Jones, R. M. (2003). Local and national ICT policies. In R. B. Kozma (ed.), *Technology, innovation, and educational change: A global perspective* (pp. 163-194). Eugene, OR: International Society for Technology in Education.

Kozma, R. B., & Voogt, J. (2003). *Technology, innovation, and educational change: A global perspective (Report of the Second Information Technology in Education*

Levy, F., & Murnane, R.J. (2004). *The new division of labor: How computers are creating the next job market.* Princeton, N.J.: Princeton University Press.

National Committee on Science, Engineering, and Public Policy. (2006). *Rising above the gathering storm: Energizing and employing America for a brighter economic future*. Washington, DC: National Academies Press.

Piaget, J. (1975). *The development of thought*. New York, NY: Viking Press.

Prensky, M. (2001). *Digital Game-Based Learning*. New York: McGraw-Hill.

Rickard, W., Oblinger, D. (2004, September 9-10, 2003). *Higher Education Leaders Symposium: Unlocking the Potential of Gaming Technology*. Paper presented at the Higher Education Leaders Symposium, Redmond, Washington.

Rieber, L. P., Smith, L., & Noah, D. (1998). The value of serious play. *Educational Technology, 38*(6), 29-37.

Squire, K. (2001). *Reframing the cultural space of computer and video games*: MIT.

Tanner, H., & Jones, S. (2000, September 7-10). *Using ICT to support interactive teaching and learning on a secondary mathematics PGCE course*. Paper presented at the British Educational Research Association (BERA), Cardiff University.

Vygotsky, L. S. (1967). Play and its role in the mental development of children. *Soviet Psychology, 5*(3), 6-18.

Wood, L. E., & Stewart, R.W. (1987). Improvement of practical reasoning skills with computer skills. *Journal of Computer-Based Instruction, 14*(2), 49-53.

Leonard A. Annetta
North Carolina State University

Meng-Tzu Cheng
North Carolina State University

NOTES

[1] http://courses.ncsu.edu/ems594/common/ignite/index.html
[2] NSF Project ESI-0525115
[3] http://ced.ncsu.edu/hifives

CHAPTER 2

21ˢᵗ Century Skills and Serious Games: Preparing the N Generation

If it were possible to define the mission of education, it could be said that its fundamental purpose is to ensure that all students benefit from learning in ways that allow them to participate fully in public, community, and economic life (New London Group, 2000, p. 9).

INTRODUCTION

Ensuring that all students have the opportunity to participate fully in society is a daunting challenge for educators. Central to this challenge in the 21ˢᵗ century is changing how we view learning. Serious games, an area that is gaining momentum in education, has potential to transform how we view learning as we meet the fast-paced, ever-changing demands of modern life. Forging a conceptual bridge between serious games and highly-valued emerging skills, this chapter: 1) defines evolving characteristics of the 21ˢᵗ century learner, 2) synthesizes proposed 21ˢᵗ century skills from different disciplines, and 3) analyzes how certain features of serious games can promote the highly valued 21ˢᵗ century skills of *expert problem-solving* and *complex communication*. The chapter closes with a call for more thoughtful empirical studies in order to establish a research base for the emerging field of serious games.

THE 21ˢᵀ CENTURY LEARNER

Today's students, commonly referred to as the N generation, millenials, or digital natives, were born into social and educational environments where digital technologies are pervasive. The emergence of this first technologically savvy generation creates new challenges for parents (e.g., monitoring time devoted to digital interactions and appropriate content) as well as for educators. Digitally native students bring different skills, interests, and needs to the classroom and educators are grappling to understand these unique attributes in order to design instruction accordingly. Many educators decry the violence and inappropriateness of content both on the web and in games, while others look past the immediate problems and see potential for educational applications. The learning principles that are embedded within games and to which they owe much of their popularity

L.A. Annetta (ed.), Serious Educational Games: From Theory to Practice, 13–23.
© *2008 Sense Publishers. All rights reserved.*

are often overlooked. As the numbers of game players increase it becomes even more important that educators find ways to harness this phenomenon for educational purposes.

Young people's enthusiasm for the Internet and video games is not a trivial trend. Over one billion people, one sixth of the world's population, were accessing the Internet in 2005 (Internet World Stats: Usage and Population Statistics, n.d.). Even a conservative estimate would suggest that nearly half of the world's population will be online within the next five years. In the U.K., 74% of children and young people aged nine to nineteen have access to the Internet at home, and most of these are daily or weekly Internet users (Livingstone & Bober, 2005). In Japan, 98% of homes have access to the Internet with broadband 16 times faster than that found in the U.S. In the US, the Pew Internet & American Life Project has conducted surveys on children and teens technology use since 2000. In the most recent survey Lenhart and Maddan (2007) reported that 93% of teens use the Internet. More than half of online teens indicated that they were creating content in the form of blogs, videos, or music.

At the state level, a recent survey was conducted of 4000 middle grades students (sixth, seventh, and eighth grades) who were in a North Carolina statewide after-school program (Spires, Lee, Turner & Johnson, 2008). This mixed-methods study included the survey as well as a sample of 48 students drawn from the larger group who participated in one-hour focus group sessions. Students reported high frequency usage of video and online games, music services as well as email, instant messaging, and cell phone services out of school. There was a difference between what students said about in school and out of school technology uses. In school students reported high levels of computer-based skills work and moderate levels of Internet-based research. Students were also asked about where they found information for completing their work and 86% of respondents indicated that they used the Web as opposed to printed materials. When asked about activities they enjoyed in school, students listed doing research on the Internet above working on projects in a group, listening to the teacher explain things, and doing worksheets. Analysis of survey data revealed no significant differences in computer usage in and out of school among ethnic groups as well as rural and non-rural students' uses of computers.

The main distinctions that emerge between in and out of school technology use relate to the intent of the technology use and the actual devices being used. Outside of school students are using technology for communication and entertainment purposes. They also are more likely to use smaller handheld and gaming devices outside of school. Inside school students are using desktop computers for web-based research, word-processing and other productivity purposes (spreadsheets, PowerPoint, etc.). The surveys suggested that students' technology use inside school is often less creative and meaningful than their technology use outside of school. Students expressed strong opinions in all the surveys about what technologies they thought should be in school and how they thought these technologies should be used, and they viewed technology skills and understandings in general as essential for their success in adult workplaces. Interestingly, research suggests that while they are frequent users of technology tools, Net-Geners typically lack information literacy skills, and their critical thinking skills are often weak (Oblinger & Oblinger, 2005). They may be digital natives, but they do not necessarily understand how their use of technology affects their ways of learning.

WHAT KNOWLEDGE AND SKILLS ARE ESSENTIAL FOR THE 21ST CENTURY?

In 1900 in his seminal essay, *What Knowledge is of Most Worth?*, social theorist Herbert Spencer stated that this question needed to be answered before designing curriculum or instruction. As we make our way into the 21st century, Spencer's provocative question is still front and center but this time in the midst of fast-paced technological changes that are driving the global economy. With ongoing advancements in information technologies creating much of the change we experience, different groups are thinking hard about the new knowledge and skills that are needed for workplace productivity. Even though it is impossible to predict the future, based on current expectations from the business community trends are emerging in terms of new skills that are needed. The Partnership for 21st Century Skills (P21) (2005) is the latest in a series of business-education consortia that have delineated core content, skills, and processes that are deemed critical to the twenty-first century workplace. P21's perspective is consistent with that of many economists and nonprofit organizations that address workforce-capacity issues (Levy & Murnane, 2004; Dede, Korte, Nelson, Valdez, & Ward, 2005). Arguing to "bridge the gap between how students live and how they learn" (p. 4), P21 has identified six key elements for 21st century education including, core subjects and learning skills as well as 21st century tools, contexts, content, and assessment. These six elements shape an educational reform agenda that P21 argues will enable young people to develop a wide range of skills (e.g., media, communication critical thinking, creative, problem solving, interpersonal, collaborative) while using information and communication technologies in real world contexts. To help education leaders and policymakers implement 21st century teaching and learning, P21 recently launched Route 21 (P21, 2007), an online, one-stop shop for 21st century skills-related information, resources and tools. Interestingly, P21's claims are similar to the SCAN report that emerged in the 1990's.

P21 suggests that technology plays an important role in educational change and much of the proposed change is tied to the tools and resources students use in their everyday lives. As reported earlier, students are becoming increasingly dependent on technologies to communicate, gather information, extend social experiences, and be entertained. Obviously, as students move into the workplace their interest in technologies transfers with them; the workplace, however, often expects workers to have even more sophisticated technological skills and know-how and a disposition receptive to change.

Coming from a popular press perspective and being more global with his concepts than P21, Daniel Pink in *A Whole New Mind*, (2005) boldly claims that "the future belongs to a very different kind of person with a very different kind of mind—creators and empathizers, pattern recognizers, and meaning makers. These people . . . will now reap society's richest rewards and share its greatest joys." (p.1). Arguing that we have already passed from the informational age to the conceptual age, Pink claims that in addition to left brain-directed reasoning, which was dominant in the information age, right-brain approaches are also essential in the conceptual age in order to be successful. Table 1 depicts the six senses that Pink asserts must prevail to be successful in today's society.

Table 1. A Whole New Mind: Moving from the Information Age to the Conceptual Age. (Pink, 2005).

Right-Brain Senses	Description
Design	Creating something aesthetically appealing, whimsical or emotionally engaging.
Story	A tool that is enriched by emotion, a deeper understanding of how we fit in the world and why that matters.
Symphony	The ability to put together the pieces; to synthesize rather than to analyze; to see relationships among unrelated fields, to detect patterns; to invent something new by combining elements nobody else thought to pair.
Empathy	Being able to discern what makes a fellow woman or man tick to forge relationships and to care for others.
Play	Ample evidence points to the enormous health and professional benefits of laughter, lightheartedness, games, and humor.
Meaning	Our abundance has freed millions of people to pursue significant desires: purpose, transcendence, and spiritual fulfillment.

Another group that has done advanced thinking in the area of 21st century skills is MIT Professor Henry Jenkins (2007) and his colleagues. The skills that Jenkins promotes are more localized to media literacies than the global skills that Pink and the P21 group target. Prompted by the rich media landscape that exists today, Jenkins has articulated a new skill set that involves social skills developed through collaboration and social networking. These skills build on the foundation of traditional literacy, research skills, technical skills, and critical analysis skills taught in the classroom. Table 2 depicts these new media literacies, which are contextualized within digital media environments. Note that both Pink and Jenkins point to "play" as a 21st century skill, although they define it in different ways (see Chapter 4 of this text for a discussion of educational play). Pink points to the health and professional byproducts of play; Jenkins, on the other hand, claims play is as an approach to problem solving. Interestingly, both authors use "empathy" and "negotiation" as very similar concepts.

Table 2. New Media Literacies (Jenkins, 2006)

New Media Literacy	Description
Play	Capacity to experiment with one's surroundings as a form of problem-solving.
Performance	Ability to adopt alternative identities for improvisation and discovery.
Simulation	Ability to interpret and construct dynamic models of real-world processes.
Appropriation	Ability to meaningfully sample and remix media content.
Multitasking	Ability to scan one's environment and shift focus as needed to salient details.
Distributed Cognition	Ability to interact meaningfully with tools that expand mental capacities.
Collective Intelligence	Ability to pool knowledge & compare notes with others toward a common goal.
Judgment	Ability to evaluate the reliability & credibility of different information sources.
Transmedia Navigation	Ability to follow the flow of stories and information across multiple modalities.
Networking	Ability to search for, synthesize, and disseminate information.
Negotiation	Ability to travel across diverse communities, discerning and respecting multiple perspectives, and grasping and following alternative norms.

Dede (2007) astutely argues that proposed skills and knowledge are not robust enough to encompass what is needed for the future; but rather *understandings* and *performances* will better serve our transition into 21st century work and life. Levy and Murnane (2004) suggest that expert thinking and complex communication are essential for contemporary work, since these are the two areas in the workplace that computers cannot replace human beings. Expert problem solving involves effective pattern matching based on detailed knowledge, metacognition, and the set of skills used by the perplexed expert to determine when to end one strategy and try the next. Complex communication involves managing multiple information streams as well as the capability to interpret subtleties and present convincing arguments. In an economy flooded with new concepts and invented language, communicating complex information effectively is an increasingly valued skill. Complex problem solving, quick and intuitive decision-making ability, collaboration skills, and resourcefulness are the keys to success in the workplace. The rapid pace of change and the need for continuous learning makes the capacity to learn a highly valued competency as well.

If we synthesize across the various taxonomies that have been described, it appears that the bottom line for 21st century life and work is that we need, first, continuous learners who can forge understandings in ambiguous and complex problem solving landscapes. Second, we need learners who can collaborate with multiple information and communication streams. In an era of high stakes testing, schools do not typically place these two performances at the center of education. The question that many educators are asking is, "How do we turn the educational corner to nurture these dispositions in our schooling process?" Multiple agendas are emerging in order to answer this question; one area that shows promise but still needs much research is the area of serious games.

HOW CAN SERIOUS GAMES ENABLE 21ST CENTURY SKILLS IN EDUCATIONAL SETTINGS?

With growing numbers of people around the world playing computer games, the economic and social implications of this phenomenon are profound. A single definition of serious games does not appear to exist, although typically the term depicts games that are used for training, advertising, simulation, or education. Educators are attempting to find ways to appropriate the best features of game-based learning and bring them into the formal classroom. Not surprisingly, the two 21st century skills of complex communication and expert problem solving are dominant features that cut across most game genres. For the most part, traditional schools are not set up to provide learning contexts that promote these two skills. Problem-based learning scenarios have been used for years to try to approximate real life problems and have met with some success in education. But typically problem-based learning modules have not approached the cognitive complexity and fast-paced processing that game contexts afford. Additionally, there is a gap between what students have a growing demand for, what our global economy requires, and what traditional schools can afford. While game-based learning will not be a singular answer to filling the gap, it can provide movement in the right direction.

The modern work environment is about managing complex information streams, which increasingly is a critical part of job performance. Games can provide a context for situated learning in which players are immersed in complex, problem solving tasks that require expertise. Examining the role of expertise in modern culture, John Bransford and his colleagues (e.g., Schwartz, Bransford, & Sears, 2005) distinguish between routine and adaptive expertise. Routine experts are adept at solving routine problems every day; adaptive experts exhibit flexibility, which is highly valued in today's workplace since knowledge and skill requirements change significantly over the course of a career. While routine experts may be efficient and technically skillful, they may not be able to flexibly adapt to solve new problems; adaptive experts are able to adapt to as well as seek out new learning situations (Hatano & Oura, 2003). Adaptive expertise is clearly a key feature of game environments.

Becker & Wade (2004) deconstruct complex communication and expert problem solving further and assert that the following characteristics of gamers map on to the needs of the 21st century workplace. Gamers are able to:

- Rapidly analyze new situations
- Interact with characters they don't really know
- Solve problems quickly and independently
- Think strategically in a chaotic world
- Collaborate effectively in teams

These characteristics are evident in commercial massively multiplayer online games (MMOGs) like *World of War Craft*, or *Everquest 2*. MMOGs share many of the same features of other games except they are played online. Steinkuehler (2004) asserts that these games can be cognitively demanding, requiring exploration of complex, multi-dimensional problem spaces, as well as empirical model building systems. These environments require the negotiation of meaning and values within the online community as well as the coordination of avatars and multiple forms of text. *Civilization III* is an example of a commercial entertainment game that provides extensive experience in problem solving. As players lead a civilization from 4000 BC to the present, they seek out geographical resources, manage complex economies, and hold diplomatic summits with other nations. Squire (2003) conducted a study to see what students learned about social studies from Civilization III, even though the game is designed primarily for entertainment. Students understood the concepts of monotheism and monarchy as well as learned how to synthesize disparate periods of history.

Becker and Wade's characteristics are also evident in non-commercial games, such as Dede's long standing *River City*, an immersive simulation for middle school students. This MUVE (Multiuser Virtual Environment) is an example of an academic enterprise that was created using designed-based research and promotes both complex communication and expert problem solving. Following the path of *River City*, with the addition of intelligent tutors, *Crystal Island*, is being developed at North Carolina State University by a team of computer scientists and educational researchers. This NSF funded project (Lester, Spires, & Nietfeld, 2007) is an example of an academic innovation that targets science education for 8th grade middle students. Taking their cues from Jerome Bruner (1990, p. 35), who observed that the way people organize their experience and knowledge with the social world "is narrative rather than conceptual," the creators used a narrative centered learning environment to explore concepts related to microbiology (Mott & Lester, 2006).

The learning environment (see Figure 1) is set on a recently discovered volcanic island where a research station has been established to study the unique flora and fauna. The user plays the role of the daughter (or son) of a visiting scientist who is attempting to discover the origins of an unidentified illness at the research station. The environment begins by introducing the student to the island and the members of the research team for which her father serves as the lead scientist. As members of the research team fall ill, it is her task to discover the cause of the outbreak. She is free to explore the world to collect physical evidence and interact with other characters. Through the course of her adventure she must gather enough evidence to correctly choose among candidate diagnoses including botulism, cholera, salmonellosis, and tick paralysis as well as identify the source of the disease relying on her knowledge of genetics to solve the mystery.

| (a) | (b) |

Figure 1: The CRYSTAL ISLAND Learning Environment

The task-oriented environment of *Crystal Island*, its semiautonomous characters, and the user interface are implemented with Valve Software's Source™ engine, the 3D game platform for Half-Life 2. The user can perform a broad range of actions including performing experiments in the laboratory, interacting with other characters, reading "virtual books" to obtain background information on diseases, and collecting data about the food recently eaten by the members of the research team. Throughout the mystery, users can walk around the island and visit the infirmary, the lab, the dining hall, and the living quarters of each member of the team. In the current test bed, there are 20 goals users can achieve, three hundred unique actions the user can carry out, and over fifty unique locations in which the actions can be performed. As a narrative centered learning environment, *Crystal Island* satisfies Malone & Leper's (1987) criteria of challenge, curiosity, control and fantasy; learning includes competence and direction in the face of novelty, complexity, and ambiguity. A series of experimental studies are underway that will assess the effects that using *Crystal Island* has on student problem solving and affect. Additionally, the research is examining how well performance in the environment predicts a range of academic dispositions (Spires, Turner, McQuiggan, & Lester, 2008; McQuiggan & Lester, 2008).

CONCLUSION

As educators continue the quest to ensure that all students have the opportunity to participate fully in society, multiple paths for learning must be explored. Although in its infancy, game-based technologies hold promise in forging new models of learning and teaching for the formal schooling process. Central to this challenge in the 21st century is finding cross-sector partners who are willing to take up the research and development mantel in order to shed more light on the educational benefits of games. Gee (2003) identified 36 learning elements embedded within games that he analyzed. He concluded: "Better theories of learning are embedded in the video games many children in elementary and high school play than in the schools they attend. Furthermore, the theory of learning in good video games fits better with the modern, high-tech global worlds of today's children and teenagers live in than do the theories (and practices) of learning they see in school" (p.7). Gee's assertion, no doubt, is designed to be provocative; but his statement holds some truth. As games become more popular, however, generalized, non-substantiated statements will not serve the field well. We need a systematic way to analyze the learning features of games and conduct educational research that will help articulate the cognitive, affective, and social benefits for education.

Gaming technology will need to overcome the same types of resistance that, in recent years, other technologies have confronted, (e.g., computers as tools for analysis and the Internet as a primary form of communication within business). As the field moves forward, essential questions for the educational research community are: What are the critical factors built into game-based environments and how can they inform our current theories of teaching and learning? How can we appropriate the very best of what games have to offer for educational purposes in the 21st century? In the best interest of the N generation and future learners to come, we need to answer these questions thoughtfully and thoroughly—and we need to answer them sooner rather than later.

REFERENCES

Becker, J. C., & Wade, M. (2004). *Got game: How the gamer generation is reshaping business forever.* Boston: Harvard Business School Press.

Bruner, J. (1990). *Acts of meaning.* Cambridge: Harvard University Press.

Dede, C. (in press). *Transforming Education for the 21st Century: New Pedagogies that Help All Students Attain Sophisticated Learning Outcomes.* Raleigh, NC: Friday Institute, North Carolina State University, in press.

Dede, C., Korte, S., Nelson, R., Valdez, G., & Ward, D. (2005). *Transforming Education for the 21st Century: An Economic Imperative.* Chicago, IL: Learning Point Associates, 2005. http://www.learningpt.org/tech/transforming.htm

Gee, J.P. (2003). *What video games can teach us about literacy and learning.* New York: Palgrave-McMillan.

Hatano, G., & Oura, Y. (2003). Reconceptualizing transfer using insight from expertise research. *Educational Researcher, 32*(8), 26-29.

Jenkins, H. (2007). *Confronting the challenges of participatory cultures: Media education for the 21st century.* MacArthur Foundation: Chicago, IL.

Lenhart, A. & Maddan, M. (2007). *Social Networking Websites and Teens: An Overview.* Retrieved April 27, 2007, from http://www.pewinternet.org/PPF/r/198/report_display.asp

Levy, F. & Murnane, R. (2004). *The new division of labor: How computers are creating the next job market.* Princeton, NJ: Princeton University Press.

Livingstone, S., & Bober, M. (2005). *UK children go online: Final report of key project findings.* Project Report. London: London School of Economics and Political Science.

Malone, T., and Lepper, M. (1987). Making learning fun: A taxonomy of intrinsic motivations for learning. In Snow, R., and Farr, M. (Eds.), *Aptitude, Learning, and Instruction: Cognitive and Affective Process Analyses* (pp. 223-253). Erlbaum, Hillsdale, NJ.

McQuiggan, S.W. & Lester, J.C. (2008, March). Affect and motivation in narrative-centered learning environments. In L. Annetta, (Chair). Motivation, Affect and Engagement in Game-Based Learning Environments. Paper to be presented as part of a symposium for the American Education Research Association. New York, NY.

Mott, B., and Lester, J. (2006). Narrative-Centered Tutorial Planning for Inquiry-Based Learning Environments. In *Proceedings of the Eighth International Conference on Intelligent Tutoring Systems,* Jhongli, Taiwan, 675-684.

New London Group (2000). A pedagogy of multiliteracies: Designing social futures. In B. Cope & M. Kalantzis, (Eds.), *Multiliteracies: Literacy Learning and the Design of Social Futures* (pp. 9-38) London: Routledge.

Oblinger D. G., & Oblinger, J. L. (2005). *Educating the net generation.* Boulder, CO: Educause.

Partnership for 21st Century Skills. (2007). *Route 21.* Retrieved Nov. 25, 2007 from http://www.21stcenturyskills.org/route21/

Pink, D. H. (2005). *A whole new mind: Moving from the information age to the conceptual age.* New York, NY: Riverhead Books.

Schwartz, D., Bransford, J., & Sears, D. (2005). Efficiency and innovation in transfer. In J. Mestre (Ed.) *Transfer of learning* (pp. 1 – 51). Greenwich, CT: Information Age Publishing.

Spires, H., Lee, J., Turner, K., & Johnson, J. (2008). Having our say: Middle grade students' perspectives on school, technologies, and academic engagement. *Journal of Research in Technology & Education, (40) 4.*

Spires, H., Turner, K. Lester, J. & McQuiggan, S. (2008, March). *Engagement, academic dispositions, and success in game-based learning environments.* In L. Annetta, (Chair). Motivation, Affect and Engagement in Game-Based Learning Environments. Paper to be presented as part of a symposium for the American Education Research Association. New York, NY.

Squire, K. (2003, April). Replaying history: Teaching social studies with Civilization III. *Paper presented at the annual meeting of the American Educational Research Association, Chicago, IL.*

Steinkuehler, C. A. (2004). Learning in massively multiplayer online games. *Paper presented at the 6th International Conference of the Learning Sciences, Mahwah, NJ.*

AFFILIATIONS

Hiller A. Spires
Professor and Senior Research Fellow
Friday Institute for Educational Innovation
College of Education
North Carolina State University

DIANE JASS KETELHUT, JODY CLARKE, BRIAN NELSON &
GEORDIE DUKAS

CHAPTER 3

*Using Multi-User Virtual Environments to Simulate Authentic Scientific
Practice and Enhance Student Engagement*

INTRODUCTION

- 1/3 of United States high school students take the traditional three years of science;
- 1/3 of all high school students only take a single year of science;
- 18% of high school seniors reach or exceed science proficiency on the NAEP;
- 7% of the global engineering bachelor degrees are awarded to United States students;
- 40% of all United States science doctorates were granted to foreign nationals;
- 5% of all doctorate-holding scientists are either African-American or Hispanic;
- 25% of all doctorate-holding scientists are women.

These statistics come from a series of reports from a widening constituency concerned with the condition of science education in the United States (National Science Foundation, 2001; Grigg, Lauko, and Brockway, 2006; Committee on Prospering in the Global Economy of the 21st Century: An Agenda for American Science and Technology, National Academy of Sciences, National Academy of Engineering, Institute of Medicine, 2007). They tell a story of America's declining level of interest and expertise in science that is both alarming and paradoxical. Teachers in practice and developmental psychologists in laboratories have found in young children the inherent curiosity about the workings of the natural world (Piaget, 1930). Yet, for some reason, American students lose this engagement before high school.

One cause may be pedagogy: science as it is presented in the typical K-12 classroom bears little resemblance to science as practiced by scientists. Though the American Association for the Advancement of Science (AAAS), the National Research Council (NRC), and the National Science Teachers Association (NSTA), amongst others, have all called for a stronger emphasis on scientific inquiry,

L.A. Annetta (ed.), Serious Educational Games: From Theory to Practice, 25–38.

replicating authentic science experience in the classroom has proven difficult due to its novelty and intense resource requirements (The National Academies, 2005).

One approach that mitigates these challenges involves situating students in these authentic practices in a multi-user virtual environment (MUVE). MUVEs are online digital worlds where multiple participants can communicate and collaborate on shared experiences. A participant takes on the identity of an avatar, one's digital persona in a virtual world, and communicates with other participants via gestures and text chat. In the graphical virtual worlds within MUVEs, participants also interact with digital artifacts and computer-based agents.

MUVEs have been used in science education to offer professional development for teachers (Annetta and Park, 2006); develop science-based activities while promoting socially responsive behavior among student participants (Kafai, 2006; Barab, Arici, & Jackson, 2005); mentor students on science fair projects (Corbit, Kolodziej, Bernstein, & McIntyre, 2006); and support situated opportunities for students to develop and practice scientific inquiry skills (Clarke, Dede, Ketelhut, Nelson, 2006; Nelson & Ketelhut; in press).

In this chapter, we describe the ways in which one educational MUVE, *River City*, can be used to engage students in authentic practices of science. After describing the design of *River City* and how it replicates the real-world practices of scientists, we will present findings indicating that students with low self-confidence in scientific inquiry make significantly larger gains in content mastery using the MUVE than those using a paper-based equivalent. Additionally, we will examine the journey of a single student from "sleeper" to scientist.

CONTEXT

Scientific Inquiry

The goal of classroom scientific inquiry has been articulated by multiple state and federal policy doctrines (AAAS, 1990, 1993; NRC, 1996). Despite this, access for many students to inquiry-based science curriculum has been limited by numerous factors, including poor teacher preparation in inquiry, lack of laboratory space and supplies, uncertified science teachers, and a culture of high stakes testing in the United States (Nelson & Ketelhut, in press).

Further complicating the situation are the students themselves. By middle school, many students have been turned off from science, believing that they cannot 'do science' (Ketelhut, 2005). This belief, termed self-efficacy, affects student behavior in the classroom, with high self-efficacy students more likely to persevere and be engaged (Pajares, 2000). Thus, even if they were offered scientific inquiry-based curricula, students with low self-efficacy would be less likely to take advantage of this opportunity.

Therefore, what's needed are curricula that can help students learn content standards via inquiry, model inquiry for struggling teachers, and enable inquiry with little reliance on costly supplies. In addition, these curricula need to include experiences that interest students and build a belief they can succeed, regardless of their initial self-efficacy. One possible solution is to deliver scientific inquiry curricula via multi-user virtual environments. This technology is familiar and engaging to students, and there is some indication that it can be used to model good scientific inquiry practices for teachers (Nelson & Ketelhut, in press). We present one such MUVE, *River City*, as an example.

Learning in the River City MUVE

River City is a middle school science curriculum designed around national content standards and assessments in biology, ecology, epidemiology, and scientific inquiry. In the curriculum, students work in teams of three to collaboratively solve the problem of why the residents of *River City* are falling ill. Students travel back in time—in the virtual world—to the period in history when scientists were just discovering bacteria.

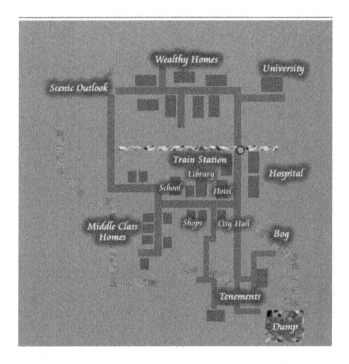

Figure 1: Map of River City

27

Figure 2: Talking to Computer-Based Agents

The curriculum is historically accurate and contains pictures from the Smithsonian Institute that help to portray an accurate picture of this time period. The three diseases (malaria, tuberculosis, and gastroenteritis) infecting the residents are similarly accurate to this time period. The *River City* virtual "world" is an industrial 19th century city with a river running through it (see Figure 1). Different forms of terrain influence water runoff in the various neighborhoods (wealthy area, middle class area and tenements). The city has a hospital, hotel, and university. The students populate the city, along with computer-based agents (residents of *River City*, see Figure 2) and digital artifacts that can include audio or video clips (such as audio clues of sick residents coughing or mosquitoes buzzing). Content in an interface-window shifts based on what the participant encounters or activates in the virtual environment (Figure 3).

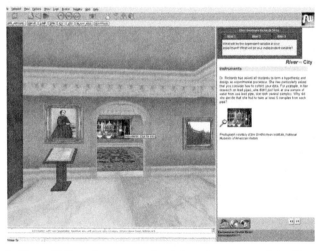

Figure 3: View of 3-D environment and web-based content on right side of screen

Inquiry and River City

Students learn to become scientists by engaging in the inquiry practices of scientists. In *River City*, students engage in all aspects of inquiry as defined by the National Science Education Standards (NRC, 1996). These aspects are listed in Table 1 below, with descriptions of how they are manifested in the *River City* curriculum (Ketelhut, 2007; Nelson & Ketelhut, in press).

Table 1: How River City Objectives Map onto Inquiry (as defined by the NRC, 1996).

Making Observations	Throughout the curriculum students are asked to make observations and draw inferences about what they see and hear as they move around the world.
Posing Questions	Students are prompted to pose questions about the problems in *River City*. They record these and reflect on them as they gather data and make observations and inferences. Students can also pose questions of the 32 computerized residents of *River City* and elicit short sets of information.
Planning Experiments	Students are guided through a generalized process of the scientific method, where they learn how to turn their questions into hypotheses and to design procedures to test those hypotheses.
Conducting Experiments	Students conduct their experiment in *River City*. They visit a 'control world' (controlled part of their experiment for gathering data), then they visit the 'experimental world' (where their independent variable has been changed and recollect the data from the same sources). They then compare the data gathered in the two worlds and write up their results using graphs and charts.
Using tools to gather data	Students use virtual microscopes (see Figure 4) to examine water purity and numbers of mosquitoes. In addition, *River City* has an Environmental Health Meter which indicates a relative level of healthiness of an area.
Communicating Results	Students write up their results in a report to the Mayor of *River City*. They also participate in a research conference where they present and share their findings with their classmates.

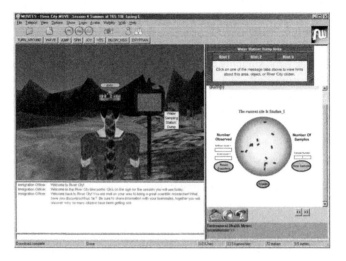

Figure 4: Taking a water sample with the virtual microscope. Students click on the "Water Sampling Station" green sign and a microscope appears in the right hand interface with moving EColi.

Advancing Through the Curriculum: Collecting Data on Change over Time and Designing and Testing an Experiment

As students move through the curriculum, they visit *River City* during 4 different time periods: October 1878, January 1879, April 1879, and July 1879. After collecting data across these 4 seasons to support their forming a data-driven hypothesis, teams of students then design their experiment face-to-face in their classroom.

Students test their hypothesis in a classic controlled experimental design. They are able to gather data in two identical worlds that only differ by one factor, their independent variable, which they choose. First, they reenter the unchanged *River City* in what is termed the 'control world.' In this world, they not only gather baseline data but tell the software what variable they want to change. After gathering their control data, students then enter a world that is identical in all aspects except for one, their independent variable. For example, if students think the illness they identified is spreading because of the mosquitoes breeding by the bog, they might choose to investigate the effects of draining the bog on illness. Thus, when they enter the experimental world the bog will appear to have been drained (see Figure 5). Students must then gather data from the same sources as they did in the control world in order to see how draining the bog affected River City. Students analyze data from their experiment by comparing their findings in each world.

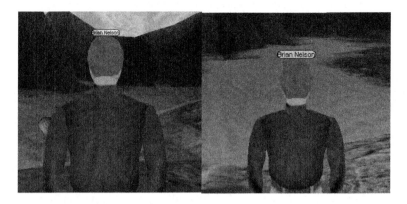

Figure 5: Student avatar observing the bog in the control world (on left) and the dried up bog in the experimental world (on the right)

Finally, students write up their research in the form of a report to the mayor of *River City*. The report, based on the concept of a lab report, describes their experiment, research findings, conclusions, and recommendations for how the mayor can stop the spread of illness in *River City*. Teams of students then present their research and findings to the entire class. The purpose of this final sharing day is to model the dissemination practice of scientists while helping students see the multivariate nature of the problem in *River City*.

RESEARCH DESIGN AND FINDINGS

Research Design

To determine whether students who participate in *River City* demonstrate greater gains in understanding the practices of scientists than students who participate in a similar paper-based curriculum and to explore how students develop a conception of themselves as inquiry learners, we examined the results of implementations held in a northeastern city in 2004 in ten middle school classes taught by a single teacher. Three classes were assigned to the non-computer control treatment, while the remainder used *River City*. A multiple-choice instrument was used to assess student knowledge of and self-efficacy in scientific inquiry, and a random subset of students were interviewed before and after implementation. Students also generated drawings of themselves at the outset and a letter to the mayor at the end that were analyzed qualitatively and rated for quantitative analysis. Additionally, students in *River City* generated data including chat transcripts, online notes, and usage log files.

How do the gains in understanding the practices of scientists for students who participate in River City compare to students who participate in a similar yet paper-based curriculum?

The content instrument consisted of multiple-choice questions assessing student understanding and knowledge of biology and scientific inquiry; twenty-two of those questions were on conceptions of scientific inquiry. These twenty-two questions ranged from asking students to differentiate between observations and inferences to interpreting experiment scenarios. Scores were computed by adding up the number of correct responses, which ranged from 0 to 22 with higher scores representing more content knowledge.

Since, as indicated earlier, self-efficacy can mediate behaviour and effort, we chose to control for students entering levels of self-efficacy in scientific inquiry. This was assessed via a twelve-item subscale on the affective measure through the Self-Efficacy in Technology and Science (SETS) instrument. Students rated each item on a scale from 1 (low) to 5 (high) as to how well that item fit them. Overall scores were computed by averaging the student's responses across the twelve items of the subscale, with high scores representing high self-efficacy to perform scientific inquiry. The measure has an estimated internal consistency reliability of .86 in a population of middle school students (Ketelhut, 2007).

Figure 6 illustrates the effect of being in the *River City* treatment on scientific inquiry gain scores, controlling for starting self-efficacy in scientific inquiry. Students who entered the project with low levels of self-efficacy did, on average, significantly better with *River City* as opposed to the control curriculum, posting gain scores of up to nearly four points with control students showing a decrease from pre to post test. However, this situation reverses at the sample self-efficacy mean. For students with average self-efficacy scores, there are no differences between the treatments, and students with starting self-efficacy scores above the mean did better in the control treatment than in *River City*.

One of our goals in creating River City was to reach the unengaged student. These results indicate that River City has the potential to do just that. We would predict that students with low self-efficacy would participate less and thus learn less than those with higher self-efficacy, and that is what we see in the paper-based curriculum. However, River City students offer the opposite scenario—as self-efficacy decreases, student gains increase. Integrating curricula such as River City with more traditional approaches offers different students the opportunity to excel.

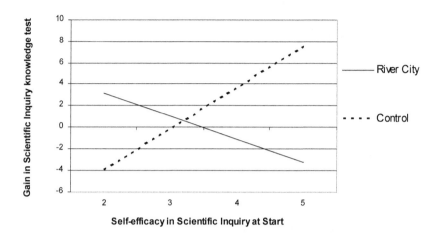

Figure 6. The Effect of River City on Gain in Scientific Inquiry knowledge, controlling for starting Self-efficacy in Scientific Inquiry (n=96).

How does one student develop his conception of himself as an inquiry learner?

To enrich the quantitative relationships shown in the section above, we offer a case study of one student to show how participating in *River City* not only builds scientific inquiry knowledge but also shapes student identity as a scientist. In this particular case, Larruge (not his real name) sheds his identity as a "student failing science" and takes on the identity of a "scientist" (Clarke, 2006).

Larruge is a 12 year old male in the 7th grade for whom English is a second language. By traditional measures, Larruge is a low-achieving student. He flunked the 7th grade and will repeat it next year. He does not think he is "good at science," has low self-efficacy, and describes the practices and activities of his science class as "boring." When asked to draw how he participates in science class, Larruge draws himself sleeping at his desk while his teacher stands in the front of the class (see Figure 7).

Teachers are asked to rate their expectations of student participation with the *River City* project on different dimensions: behavior, engagement, and content mastery. Larruge's teacher rated him a 3 out of 5 for both content mastery and behavior and a 2 for engagement. Larruge's non-participation in science and with his teachers places him at a peripheral role in his science class. Would participating in *River City* change any of that?

Figure 7: Larruge doing science in school

Generally, students spend the first day of the project getting acclimated to the virtual world and figuring out how to communicate with each other and with the *River City* residents. However, Larruge starts atypically. He enters *River City* and immediately starts organizing his teammates:

Larruge*:*   Hey Tk2 since were team mates we need to decide where to meet so we can work together okay write back.

On his second day in *River City*, Larruge organizes his team again and starts to engage in practices of a scientist: making observations and inferences and sharing this research with his teammates:

Larruge: Hey, I think that people are getting sick during the summer more than winter.
Jessica: Did you guys talk to anyone?
Larruge: I got it from Miss Howell
Larruge: Ya and
Jessica: What did they say

Larruge:	She told me that people get better in the winter. It's maybe because people don't go out in the summer.
Larruge:	So people what did you find out?
Jessica:	I talked to Nurse Jensen she's in the hospital
Larruge:	Ohh, what did she say
Jessica:	She said that the people in the hospital are complaining of a bad cough

In addition to sharing observations and inferences, Larruge and his team become curious and act on their curiosity:

Tk2:	The cook said people are really liking his food now
Larruge:	I know I talked to him
Larruge:	Hey so what you find out Tk2
Jessica:	Dr. Wright said that most of the people that are sick because of insects
Tk2:	Erica has a bad fever and her mom thinks it's from the bog
Larruge:	Bog? Who's Erica
Tk2:	I am going to the bog
Larruge:	Hold on I'm going with you okay
Larruge:	Jessica we're going to the bog

Through his interactions with the environment and then his teammates, we see how Larruge struggles with the problem and makes sense of complexity. In the experimental world, Tk2 is confused about where the trash went, and Larruge explains what happened. Through this interaction, Larruge demonstrates his understanding of their problem solving:

Larruge:	Okay so that happened; the streets are clean and so is the river
Tk2:	The trash goes to the sea
Larruge:	No No
Larruge:	Its so clean
Tk2:	Yeah but why
Larruge:	Because the people cleaned the city
Tk2:	The ocean?????/
Larruge:	No the city and because the city was clean when it [trash] doesn't go in to the water
Larruge:	So I'm going to the hospital

One of the key elements of collaborative learning in situated environments is that groups can draw out misconceptions and ineffective strategies (Brown, Collins, Duguid, 1989). We see that this team's collaboration and discussion helps Tk2 uncover his misconception about what happened. In further discussion, Larruge offers an explanation and ties it back to their experiment, offering a causal reason that the trash is no longer going into the water.

Science advances through curiosity, and thus fostering scientific habits of mind involves fostering curiosity (AAAS, 1993). While there is often little room for curiosity in traditional schooling, environments like *River City* can foster this. Through the chat transcripts, we see that Larruge's path is often driven by his curiosity. This frames his transformation to a scientist who is engaged in inquiry. This is quite different from his pre-interview, when Larruge said he was often "bored" in science class. In the post-interview, Larruge says that *River City* was so "fun" that he did not feel like he was "in class."

> Like, we were learning stuff without trying a lot. So, I learned what a thing was, what's it called, not an observation but..[an inference]. Yeah. It's um what you think is happening when you make an observation.

Although he said he was "learning stuff without trying a lot," later in the post-interview, Larruge says he was "trying so hard to figure out why they were getting sick." He further elaborates that he felt like a "scientist":

> Oh, I don't know, I guess that um the reason I liked it I guess cause you know I got to be a scientist in it. (Laughs). So, I am not really that smart either so it was kind interesting.

While Larruge still does not think he is "smart," he does say he felt "a little more" different about his ability to do science. Not only does he want to go to science class, but it "got students thinking" and "interested in science." "Thinking more" provided a challenge--it was not too easy—and also gave a sense of ownership for what his team "thought" about the problem.

As illustrated through his trajectory, Larruge's participation in the valuable social practice of *River City* leads to the development of his identity as a self-directed learner (Greeno, 1997). Additionally, according to the pre-post content measures, Larruge improves his biology knowledge by 20% and his inquiry skills by 22%; his letter to the mayor receives a score of 7 out of 9. These results support what we are seeing by mapping his trajectory of participation in the *River City* project. This is the same student who, when asked to draw a picture of science class in the pre-interview, drew himself sleeping in class and stated, "I'm slow at this stuff."

CONCLUSIONS

Creating a generation of students who find science interesting and a potential career path involves re-thinking how we teach science in K-12 classrooms. *River City* is not a panacea, nor are MUVEs and/or video games. However, what we have shown is that MUVEs, when designed around inquiry and science standards, have the potential to engage students in participating in the processes of science, particularly low-achieving students.

Bruce M. Alberts, chair of the National Research Council, stated in 1995,

"We've managed to turn people off of science by making it some kind of rote learning exercise" ("Panel Urges Shift of Focus for School Science Courses," 1995). Unless we find a way to reverse this, the trends shown in the statistics at the start of this chapter will continue downhill. We need to explore new pedagogies, such as *River City*, to make science more accessible for all.

REFERENCES

American Association for the Advancement of Science. (1990). *Science for all Americans*. New York: Oxford University Press.

American Association for the Advancement of Science. (1993). *Benchmarks for science literacy: A Project 2061 report*. New York: Oxford University Press.

Annetta, L. & Park, J.C. (2006). *Video games in science: A model for students and teachers creating 3d role playing games*. Paper presented at the Annual Conference of the Society for Information Technology and Teacher Education, Orlando, FL.

Barab, S., Arici, A., & Jackson, C. (2005). Eat your vegetables and do your homework: a design based investigation of enjoyment and meaning in learning. *Educational Technology*, 45(1), 15-20.

Brown, J. S., Collins, A., & Duguid. (1989). Situated Cognition and the Culture of Learning. Educational Researcher, 18(1), 32-42.Business Higher Education Forum. (2005). *A commitment to America's Future: Responding to the crisis in mathematics and science education*. Available: http://www.bhef.com/MathEduReport-press.pdf [2005, July].

Clarke, J. (2006). *Making learning meaningful: An exploratory study of using MUVEs to teach middle school science*. Unpublished Qualifying Paper presented to the Harvard Graduate School of Education, Cambridge, MA.

Clarke, J., Dede, C., Ketelhut, D. J., & Nelson, B. (2006). A design-based research strategy to promote scalability for educational innovations. *Educational Technology, 46* (3), 27–36.

Committee on Prospering in the Global Economy of the 21st Century: An Agenda for American Science and Technology, National Academy of Sciences, National Academy of Engineering, Institute of Medicine. (2007). R*ising above the gathering storm: Energizing and employing America for a brighter economic future*. Washington, DC: The National Academies Press.

Corbit, Margaret, S. Kolodziej, R. Bernstein and C. McIntyre. (May 2006) Student Project Virtual Worlds as Windows on Scientific Cultures in Proceedings of the 9th International Conference on Public Communication of Science and Technology, Seoul, Korea.

Greeno, J. G. (1997). On claims that answer the wrong question. *Educational Research, 26*(1), 5-17.

Grigg, W., Lauko, M., and Brockway, D. (2006). The Nation's Report Card: Science 2005 (NCES 2006-466). U.S. Department of Education, National Center for Education Statistics. Washington, D.C.: U.S. Government Printing Office.

Kafai, Y. B. (2006). Playing and making games for learning: Instructionist and constructionist perspectives for game studies. *Games and Culture, 1*(1), 36–40.

Ketelhut, D. J. (2007). The impact of student self-efficacy on scientific inquiry skills: An exploratory investigation in River City, a multi-user virtual environment. *Journal of Science Education and Technology*, 16(1), 99-111.

Ketelhut, D. J. (2005, April 4-8). *Assessing scientific and technological self-efficacy: A measurement pilot*. Paper presented at the National Association for Research in Science Teaching, Dallas.

National Research Council. (1996). *National Science Education Standards: observe, interact, change, learn*. Washington, DC: National Academy Press.

National Science Foundation. (2001). *Characteristics of doctoral scientists and engineers in the United States, 2001*. National Science Foundation. Retrieved March 19, 2004, From: http://www.nsf.gov/sbe/srs/nsf03310/pdf/tab6.pdf.

Nelson, B., Ketelhut, D. J. (in press). Designing for real-world inquiry in virtual environments. *Educational Psychology Review*.

Pajares, F. (2000). Schooling in America: Myths, mixed messages, and good intentions (Lecture): Emory University, Cannon Chapel.

Panel Urges Shift of Focus for School Science Courses. (1995, December 7). *New York Times*. (p. 20)

Piaget, J. (1930). The child's conception of physical causality. London: K. Paul, Trench, & Trubner.

The National Academies. (2005). U.S. High School Science Lab Experiences Often Poor, But Research Points Way to Improvements. Retrieved August 2005, From: http://www4.nationalacademies.org/news.nsf/isbn/0309096715?OpenDocument.

Diane Jass Ketelhut
Temple University

Jody Clarke
Harvard University

Brian C. Nelson
Arizona State University

Geordie Dukas
Harvard University

SHAWN Y. HOLMES & BARBI HONEYCUTT

CHAPTER 4

Educational Play

INTRODUCTION

The role of play in society is complex and varied. Many behaviorists, psychologists, sociologists and educators have studied the role of play in physical, social, emotional, and cognitive development (Brougere, 1999, Edginton, et al., 2006, Rieber, 1996). In particular, educators have been interested in understanding how play can enhance learning, and with today's increased emphasis on video games and technology by students of all ages, there is renewed interest in designing learning environments around the concept of play.

The purpose of this chapter is to explore the concept of play from theoretical, educational and developmental perspectives in an effort to present educational game designers with a foundation for designing Serious Games for specific audiences. The chapter begins with an overview of the definition and characteristics of play followed by a brief discussion of how people learn. The chapter concludes with a discussion of how Piaget's stages of cognitive development can be integrated with common play theories to enhance learning in gaming environments.

DEFINITIONS AND CHARACTERISTICS OF PLAY

Play is a difficult concept to define and categorize, however, by understanding the motivations for why people play, game designers can enhance the gaming experience and align the goals of gaming for the purposes of education and learning. First, it is helpful to understand some of the general characteristics of play as defined by Edgington (2006):

- Play is generally regarded as not being instrumental in purpose.
- Play is often carried out in the spirit of pleasure and creative expression.
- Play can be aimless, disorganized, and casual, or highly structured and complex.
- Play is commonly thought of as an activity engaged in by children, but adults also play.
- Play is instinctual, although some play behavior is learned.

L.A. Annetta (ed.), Serious Educational Games: From Theory to Practice, 39–45.

- Play is voluntary and pleasurable, although it may involve risk and intense commitment.
- Play appears to be found in all cultures.

When referring to play specifically in educational settings, it is essential to design the activity based upon a clear purpose and stated learning objectives. Not all play is beneficial, and when this type of play interferes with the goal of learning, then the use of educational games can impede the potential for cognitive development.

Before moving on to the specifics of cognitive development theory, game designers need to understand that learning is defined as both a product and as a process. When referring to educational games, it is essential to examine the learning process that occurs through the playing of the game to ensure the educational goals were met.

Behaviorists and psychologists view learning as a change in behavior resulting from an experience, which results in new knowledge (Leamnson, 1999). Change in behavior can be observed or measured to illustrate that learning has indeed occurred. However, some processes, such as conditioning or habitual repetition, result in behavioral changes, but not necessarily as the result of an experience that generated or was predicated on new knowledge (Milhollan & Forisha, 1972). Additionally, we should question whether or not learning has occurred when the change in behavior is not actually demonstrated or performed.

Some researchers argue that learning can occur in the way an individual thinks about an idea, even if he or she has not had the opportunity to demonstrate the new knowledge. Many theorists focus on the individual processes in which people make sense of information, integrate that information, and possibly generate new knowledge from an experience (Milhollan & Forisha, 1972, Rogers, 1969). Placing emphasis on the process rather than the product presents opportunities for viewing learning from a developmental perspective, emphasizing positive growth and change resulting from experiences and reflection. It is highly recommended that games in any educational setting be followed by reflection or debriefing to ensure the learning objectives were accurately met. Reflections can be used as a way to anchor the experiences of the learner (Rieber, 2001).

Cognitive Development and Play Theory

One approach to understanding how to integrate play and learning is to combine Piaget's stages of cognitive development with common play theories. Integration of Piaget's developmental stages with play theories allows game designers several perspectives to consider when designing games as effective learning tools.

There are over twenty theories of play, reinforcing the notion that play is a complex term to define. This chapter will highlight some of the more well-known theories in relation to the stages of cognitive development, but it should be understood that the play theories are not exclusive to one age group or another and the theories can overlap with one another to explain the motivation for why an individual seeks to play.

One theory of play is the cognitive developmental theory which suggests that play behavior is based upon an individual's cognitive stage of development, reinforcing the concepts that play changes throughout an individual's lifetime (Edginton, et al, 2006). This developmental theory of play is connected to Piaget's research. Piaget (1969) describes play as a vehicle for interacting with the environment and proceeding through the stages of cognitive development via adaptation and assimilation. Play is an activity whose purpose is the assimilation of reality to the player. In the context of education and defined in these terms, play transforms reality by assimilation to the needs of the player, whereas imitation is accommodation to external representations. Intelligence amounts to an equilibration between assimilation and adaptation which can be achieved through play.

Piaget's categories of play; exercise play, symbolic play, games with rules, and games of construction, describe how a player evolves cognitively through adaptation and assimilation. The fourth category, games of construction, is the transition between symbolic play and non-playful activities or "serious" adaptations (Piaget & Inhelder, 1969). Play of this type initially starts with symbolism, however shifts to genuine adaptation or solutions to problems and intelligent creations. Piaget associates play to his theory of cognitive development (Huitt & Hummel, 2003) and closely relates cognitive development to his theory of adaptation (Lutz & Huitt, 2004). It is difficult to speak of one without relating it to the other.

The close association between play and cognitive development allows educators, game designers and researchers a foundation from which to use Piaget's stages as a framework for linking play to Serious Education Games. In an empirical meta-analysis study of the impact of computer use on preschooler's social, cognitive, language development and motivation, McCarrick and Li (2007) associate their findings with the frameworks of Erikson, Piaget, and Vygotsky. Specifically concerning Piaget's theories, one study assessed children's at home computer use. This study noted children with computer access scored significantly higher on cognitive and school readiness assessments. In a second study children were pretested and posttested for intelligence, creativity and self-esteem. Children using the developmentally appropriate software with supplemental activities scored significantly higher on posttests for six out of eight cognitive subtests. Children also using developmentally appropriate software without supplemental activities gained in cognitive skills on four out of eight of the cognitive assessments (McCarrick & Li, 2007). Both studies suggest support for computer use as a means to engage children in active learning. The use of developmentally appropriate software suggests support for the association of computer software to cognitive levels.

Combining Piaget's descriptors of play with the cognitive growth that may occur by cycling through adaptation and assimilation noted as disequilibrium

(Piaget, 1975) can provide a solid structure for designing Serious Gaming environments.

Embedded in each of Piaget's stages of cognitive development are three types of knowledge: physical, logical-mathematical, and social. Physical knowledge is achieved through direct contact with the environment; logical-mathematical is obtained through actions and is achieved by thinking abstractly; and social knowledge is culture specific since it is gained through interactions with others (Lutz & Huitt, 2004). Serious Educational Game designers can support their software development with supplemental activities that provide a hands-on experience, implement multiple settings for mental structures to undergo assimilation and adaptation, and finally incorporate the multiplayer functionality.

SENSORIMOTOR STAGE

The four stages of cognitive development are age dependent and based on cognitive skill (Huitt & Hummel, 2003). The first cognitive development stage, sensorimotor, is where the child constructs a decentered and objective universe making a progression of attachments to other persons. Play at this stage, and thus intelligence, is recognized through motor activity progressing from spontaneous and reflex movements.

PRE-OPERATIONAL STAGE

During early childhood the pre-operational stage consists of the child using symbols, language, memory and imagination. This stage is also characterized by symbolic play where assimilation is made possible by language that is developed by the child and modified as needed (Piaget & Inhelder, 1969). Piaget states that a child is egocentric in the pre-operational stage and the idea of interacting with other players is not possible. The Pre-Exercise Theory supports this stage of Piaget's cognitive development. The Pre-Exercise Theory explains that play is instinctual and prepares children for future roles as adults (Edginton, et al, 2006). When children "play house" or make "mud pies" they are pretending to assume the roles and responsibilities they will encounter as adults. Educational games designed for this audience should include symbols, language, and scenarios that capture the player's instinctual need to prepare for future responsibilities. Children in the pre-operational stage are egocentric thus single player educational games, many manufactured by Scholastic® where children learn colors, numbers, or names of objects that are present in the real-world.

CONCRETE OPERATIONAL STAGE

Elementary aged children through early adolescence are in the concrete operational stage. The correlated play category is games with rules where the child uses logic and the manipulation of symbols to show cognitive development as they are related to concrete objects. For example, playing marbles allows for an opportunity to increase social life skills. Rules are socially transmitted during this type of play. Understanding rules as a child leads to the ability to use them as an adult. Play controlled by rules is where children learn social interactions and the acquisition of rules can be the start of morality. The disequilibrium present between personal rules and social rules is transmitted and resolved during this type of play. The Achievement-Motivation Theory supports this stage of cognitive development. Within this theory, the player is motivated by the desire to achieve, excel, master, and succeed (Edginton, 2006). The player usually seeks risk and competition, and the reward may be internal, such as increased self-confidence, or external, such as winning a trophy. Many of the VTech® early childhood games and those made by LeapFrog© are good examples of successful games that reach concrete operational children.

FORMAL OPERATIONAL STAGE

The formal operational stage is the final cognitive development stage occurring during the teen years where there is a logical use of symbols and is related to abstract thinking. Play in this stage moves out of symbolic play into games of construction where it advances to solutions of problems and intelligent conceptualizations. There are two play theories that relate to this developmental stage: The Optimal Arousal Theory and the Conflict-Enculturation Theory. The Optimal Arousal Theory explains that the need for play includes complexity, novelty, and dissonance (Edginton, 2006). Players seek stimulation from the environment, and need new problems to solve, and interesting places to explore.

The Conflict-Enculturation Theory explains that players seek an environment where they can become involved in new situations and learn new skills with a minimum of emotional risk (Edginton, 2006). The players seek to learn skills such as cooperation, competition, handling intense feelings, or understanding difficult situations without the risk of embarrassment, injury, or harm to the self. Adolescents may become embarrassed to directly confront aspects of themselves of a physical or social nature (Millians, 1999). Game designers must take care to craft situations where students can comfortably engage in the game, one resolution is to base the game on older or younger individuals. Popular activities might include simulations, role-plays, strategy and other experiential activities to immerse the player in the reality of the experience. Several commercial games can be implemented into the classroom for formal operational students. Role-playing examples include *Roller Coaster Tycoon* and *Cruise Ship Tycoon*, learners are engineers where they not only build structures to different specifications they manage the business revenues, develop business plans and submit safety reports. Simulations and strategy games that are fit this developmental stage and are also linked to classroom content include *SimCity* teaching civil engineering and government, and *Age of the Empires* teaching history in a specific time period.

Finally, there are two additional play theories that cross all age groups and developmental stages: the Recreation Theory and the Catharsis Theory. These two theories explain other motivations for why people engage in play. The Recreation Theory explains that the need to play stems from the need to restore or rejuvenate oneself when fatigued (Edginton, 2006). For example, when children have been in school sitting at a desk all day, then they run to the playground to re-create themselves and restore their energy before beginning their homework assignment. The purpose of play goes beyond simply having fun. Play becomes a necessary task to achieve balance. Depending on the age and preference sports, puzzle, action, adventure, role-playing, or strategy video games can be played for recreation as well as mastery.

The Catharsis Theory of play explains that play is a way to vent emotions and purge antisocial tendencies (Edginton, 2006). For example, if a teenager is frustrated or angry about a situation, he or she may take a kickboxing class to vent the anger in a socially acceptable manner. Sometimes playing videogames with fighting scenes or car chasing scenes could also satisfy this need for purging negative energies. In this case, play becomes a socially acceptable outlet for potentially harmful or destructive behaviors. The Wii™ is a seventh generation video game manufactured by Nintendo® that features the Wii™ Remote, a handheld controller that detects its position and acceleration in three dimensions. Using the Wii™ to replicate the movements during a golf swing, tennis swing or boxing match can vent emotions in an acceptable safer manner.

CONCLUSION

Play becomes purposeful and has a significant role in the development of a child's mind (Verenikina, Harris, & Lysaght, 2003). During the elementary years the Achievement-Motivation Theory states children engage in play to excel and master. Play, from Piaget's perspective, becomes a vehicle for interactions between the child and the environment. The cognitive stages allow the child to interact and adapt to its environment. The adaptation of knowledge about the environment becomes manipulated into cognitive structures. The Pre-Exercise Theory supports this stance as play is natural and children engage in make-believe play. A discrepancy between the child's knowledge about the environment and the environment itself leads to assimilation and/or accommodation (Piaget, 1975). Critics of Piaget suggest his theories provide a good framework for learning from computers; however the individualist nature of his theories may not be applicable to educational environments such as school settings (McCarrick & Li, 2007). Conversely, gaming is important for individual learning because one can choose an activity and meet a challenge without real consequence (Corbeil, 1999). The Optimal Arousal Theory and the Conflict-Enculturation Theory are good illustrations of learners needing to be challenged with intricate environments and original problems to unravel as dissonance helps them to learn new skills.

In the Recreation and Catharsis Theories video games serve the purpose of restoring balance and venting emotions in an enjoyable manner. Gaming becomes a safe environment for curiosity, challenges, having the ability to investigate, discover, and change variables, usually without true danger.

A simulation is a dynamic model of reality, dynamic in the ability to change variables if desired and a model because it is abstract in nature and represents aspects of reality (Corbeil, 1999). A learning environment where the player is successful working out rules to control a specific domain is a gaming environment. Serious Games have innovative abilities to use Piaget's cognitive development framework aligned with his theory of play as well as other play theories, which are embedded in how an individual interacts with his/her environment and is a representation of intelligence, and leverage this with an immersive power to enhance learning.

REFERENCES

Brougere, G. (1999). Some elements relating to children's play and adult simulation/gaming. *Simulation and Gaming, 30*(2), 134-146.

Edginton, C., DeGraff, D., Dieser, R., & Edginton, S. (2006). *Leisure and life satisfaction: Foundational perspectives*. 4th ed. Boston: McGraw-Hill.

Huitt, W., & Hummel, J. (2003). Piaget's theory of cognitive development. *Educational Psychology Interactive* Retrieved June 10, 2007, from chiron.valdosta.edu/whitt/col/cogsys/piaget

Leamnson, R. (1999). *Thinking about teaching and learning: Developing habits of learning with first year college and university students*. Sterling, VA: Stylus Publishing, Inc.

Piaget, J. (1975). *The development of thought*. New York: Viking Press.

Piaget, J., & Inhelder, B. (1969). *The psychology of the child*. New York: Basic Books, Inc.

Rieber, L. (1996) Seriously considering play: Designing interactive learning environments based on the blending of microworlds, simulations, and games. *Educational Technology Research and Development, 44*(2), 43-58. Retrieved June 20, 2007 from http://search.ebscohost.com/login.aspx?direct=true&db=eric&AN=EJ526319&site=ehost-live&scope=site

Rogers, C. (1969). *Freedom to learn*. Columbus, OH: Charles E. Merrill Publishing Company.

Verenikina, I., Harris, P., & Lysaght, P. (2003). *Child's play: Computer games, theories of play and children's development*. Paper presented at the IFIP Working Group 3.5 Conference, UWS Paramatta.

Shawn Y Holmes
College of Science, Mathematics and Technology Education,
North Carolina State University

Barbi Honeycutt
The Faculty Center for Teaching and Learning
North Carolina State University

ERIC N. WIEBE

CHAPTER 5

Data Visualization and Gaming

INTRODUCTION

Data visualization and gaming have common roots in the quest for the creation of high performance multi-modal interfaces to information. This chapter will explore the research and practitioner literature in educational and human factors psychology as well as information design as it relates to the design of educational gaming environments. Particular themes of interest in this chapter will be: 1) the perceptual and cognitive basis of information display, 2) user task and information display design interactions and 3) data-based learning in education. The chapter will conclude by discussing data visualization and gaming and its implication for the design of learning environments.

The use of scientific and technical data has been part of the instructional process in these fields for as long as they have existed. An equally long tradition has been to represent this data in a graphical form as an alternative representation to numeric/textual forms (Jacques Bertin, 1983; MacEachren, 1995; Tufte, 1983). In the last 20 years, increased computing capability has opened new venues for graphical representation of data (Card, Mackinlay, & Shneiderman., 1999; McCormick, Defanti, & Brown, 1987). Of particular interest here is how these information and computing technologies (ICT) have created the potential for new ways of integrating data-based thinking via graphic visualization into instruction (Cunningham, Brown, & McGrath, 1990; Friedman & diSessa, 1999; Gilbert, 2005; Gordin, Edelson, & Gomez, 1996; Wiebe, 1992; Wiebe, Clark, & Hasse, 2001). ICT has not only made traditional forms of data visualization (e.g., charts and graphs) faster and easier, but it has also opened the door for thinking about new types of data-based learning contexts. Increased ICT capabilities have meant that more immersive environments are possible through real-time updating of graphic displays driven by user feedback. While interactive, immersive graphics in data visualization has been explored in both work and instructional contexts for some time (Brown, Earnshaw, Jern, & Vince, 1995; Card et al., 1999; Mary Hegarty, 2004), the implications of these technologies in the classroom are just beginning to be explored. Indicative of the relative newness of this educational research is that data visualization research has been limited to a relatively narrow set of contexts. For example, parallel with the interest in data visualization in instructional contexts has been the rapid rise in the interest in how gaming

L.A. Annetta (ed.), Serious Educational Games: From Theory to Practice, 47–55.

technologies can be incorporated in the classroom (Kafai, 2006; Kafai, Franke, Ching, & Shih, 1998). Many of the same technologies make data visualization and gaming systems possible yet there has been little work on linking the two technologies together.

Given that the merging of data visualization and gaming in instructional settings is more a concept at this point with essentially no actualized examples, this chapter will focus on key issues surrounding the use of scientific and technical data visualization in instructional settings and then link them to similar issues in gaming—in this text and others.

A TASK ANALYSIS APPROACH

A useful starting point for exploring how data visualization and gaming might come together in a potent instructional environment is to apply task analysis, a popular methodology used by the human factors and human-computer interaction research communities (Mirel, 1998; Shah, Freedman, & Vekiri, 2005; Shneiderman, 1998). Using such an approach, some of the key factors will be to not only define what the learning tasks students will be undertaking, but also the overall context of these tasks and the capabilities (i.e., individual differences) that the learners possess. One approach would be to start with the assumption that the gaming environment will be the dominating context and that the data visualization will be one of many tools that learner employ within the gaming environment. For example, a problem-solving and/or competitive gaming environment may be defined where the learner needs to acquire certain knowledge in order to solve a problem or answer a question in order to achieve some goal within the game. Acquiring the necessary knowledge may be facilitated by manipulating data sets using visualization tools in order to understand relationships within the information. There will, of course, be exceptions to this hierarchy. So, if depicting the data as a 3D virtual space or object is determined to be the best way to represent the data, the data display and the overall gaming environment may become one in the same.

To continue on this example, the learner might need to apply principles of physics to control a space ship they are piloting; not unlike the popular 1980's game *Asteroids*. Data visualizations of velocity and location over time on the ship's control panel may be used along with a student's knowledge of Newtonian mechanics to make informed decisions about how to adjust the trajectory of the ship. Interacting with the ship's controls, altering the data values being displayed, and integrating this information with other changes in the gaming environment creates an potentially powerful learning cycle that can evolve a student's schema about Newtonian mechanics. More challenging might be to have the student determine what data variables to display and how to best display them. This example defines a goal-oriented, information seeking environment (Marchionini, 1995) in which both the innate and acquired abilities that the learner currently possess will guide how the data visualization tools within the game should be designed. It will be assumed that of primary interest is the design of data visualizations that serve active information seeking on the part of the learner. In doing so, this chapter will not directly address other aspects of information display that serves purposes such as alerts/warnings or graphics used for purely aesthetic or entertainment ends.

When looking at what the learner "brings to the table" when engaged in a gaming environment, it is important to distinguish between abilities to acquire information from graphic displays that we might consider innate and those that are learned. That is, what capabilities and behaviors can be assumed in the majority of the human population by early adolescence regardless where they grew up and what educational opportunities they had. Often these "hard-wired" visual capabilities are called one's perceptual abilities and distinguished from cognitive abilities. Cognitive abilities, as defined here, have a historical basis in what an individual experienced and how these experiences interacted with their genetically determined capabilities over the course of their life. These cognitive abilities typically will have a much wider range in the adolecent learner population than one's perceptual abilities. In designing for majority populations, perceptual abilities are typically taken as a given while cognitive abilities are (hopefully) accounted for through supporting adaptive elements internal or external to the gaming environment. Another important consideration is what special needs populations are you also going to accommodate with the design. These populations may not have the perceptual abilities of the majority population; e.g., they may be color blind. This next section will look at both these perceptual and cognitive factors.

PERCEPTUAL FACTORS

The perceptual abilities that are probably of most interest are visual characteristics that allow an individual to distinguish similarities or differences between multiple graphic elements or the ability to discern change from some previous state (Kaiser & Proffitt, 1989; MacEachren, 1995; Morse, 1979; Shah & Hoeffner, 2002). Here, the goal is to use perceptual qualities of an object to represent data values. These data values might be continuous variables such as the current velocity of an object or categorical variables based on some other quality. For example in a world map display, color might be used to code which countries are rich in petroleum resources. The context in which we talk about these visual qualities, while it has some overlap (Livingston, Sandals, & Vickers, 1992), is separate from many of the visual qualities that game designers are interested in for creating photo-realistic virtual environments. So, for example, the same qualities of color that facilitate perceiving 3D form on the computer screen (an important consideration in many gaming environments) is often leveraged in much different ways to help visually code abstract scientific data.

The perceptual quality most often manipulated in contemporary ICT data displays is color (Truckenbrod, 1981; Xing, 2006). While there are many ways of modeling color, from an information display standpoint, the most useful way of thinking about color is as being composed of three unique descriptive components or dimensions: hue, saturation, and value (Bertin, 1983; Bertoline & Wiebe, 2005) Hue can be thought of as the way we most commonly refer to color: red, green, blue, purple, etc. Hue is determined by the mixture of visible light wavelengths emanating from the object. Saturation is determined by the ratio of intensity of visible light wavelengths. The more a color has a single dominant wavelength, the more "pure" or saturated the color is. The less dominant a single wavelength is, the less saturated the color until at an even distribution of wavelengths, the color is a gray (i.e., completely desaturated). Value (sometimes called lightness or brightness) is the overall intensity of the color—the more intensity, the lighter the color. With desaturated colors, a high intensity but even mix of wavelengths will approach white while the total lack of any light energy will approach black. Though computer software (and their interfaces) will often generate colors based on a mix of the three light primaries—red, green and blue—it is still more useful to design displays based on changes in hue, saturation and value.

Colors that have similar qualities based on this model will tend to be perceptually grouped together while those that vary markedly in any of these three dimensions will typically not be. In order to create distinctions between elements in a display, all three dimensions do not all have to be varied. Variations based just on shifts in hue are quite effective as are shifts based on saturation and value or both. Because hue and saturation/value are treated as perceptually unique, they can be manipulated separately to represent two different data dimensions. For example in a simulation of a chemical reaction tank, hue might represent temperature while saturation/value might represent pressure. Saturation and value, while unique dimensions of color, are typically not used to represent different data dimensions because they are easily perceptually confused with each other. In a gaming environment, another important factor is to consider how else color is being used in the environment. For example, changes in value (i.e., lightness or darkness) are most often used to represent 3D characteristics of an object since this mimics objects in the real world. Since virtual 3D objects in a gaming environment will change value depending on the surfaces' orientation in space (that may be continually changing), it is best to avoid value in this situation to also code a data dimension.

Other common visual characteristics for encoding data include size, location, pattern, shape, and orientation (Bertin, 1981; Bertin, 1983; Cleveland, 1985; Cleveland & McGill, 1985). Size and location are particularly important and most commonly associated with traditional data visualization techniques such as charts and graphs where data variables are mapped to one, two, or three axes in space. Data values are represented by graphic objects (e.g., points, lines, bars) along these axes. When talking about data visualizations of this sort, size and location are often grouped together simply because the location of a data value in a display is often measured relative to another data point or an axis origin. Location takes on different meanings when the data includes geospatial data where two or three of the data dimensions represent physical dimensions in space. These types of visualizations encompass what we commonly refer to as maps, but the same techniques can also apply to more abstract or imaginary spaces. The geospatial dimensions in a gaming environment might be the inside of a human cell or a space station circling the moon.

One of the challenges of using size or location for encoding data dimensions is that these qualities are often perceptually calculated through multiple pieces of visual information, where assumption errors on one or more of these information sources can lead to misperceptions about size or location (Gogel, 1978). This is a problem that is particularly acute in the types of simulated 3D environments used in gaming. In the real world, the farther an object is away from us, the smaller an area on the retina on the eye it stimulates. However, we are able to transform this direct stimulus on the eye into a perceived true size of an object by coordinating other perceptual and cognitive information we have about the object. If, however, we misperceive the location of an object in space (easier to do in a simulated computer environment), we may then misjudge its size or vice versa. Even in traditional 2D data displays, perceptual errors of size and location can be made based on the amount of supporting information in the visual field. While there are ways of mitigating the chance for error, including the use of text labels indicating numeric values, many of these techniques add visual clutter or reduce the ability to holistically synthesize large amounts of data—often the goal in using graphic data visualization techniques in the first place.

COGNITIVE FACTORS

As mentioned earlier, prior experience and its influence on cognitive abilities will also influence the design of data visualizations in games (Shah & Hoeffner, 2002). Understanding the likely range of abilities of learners using a game can be important in the assumptions made during the design phase. One way of defining experience will be along three interrelated dimensions: experience with the types of data representations, experience with the underlying scientific and technical concepts generating the data set, and knowledge of elements of the game environment. To return to the earlier example of piloting a ship in a game, the learner might have past experience with bar graphs representing the velocity of the ship and with the types of map representations being used to indicate the location and orientation of the ship. Separate from familiarity with these general data representations, the user may have previously studied Newtonian mechanics in school and, therefore, understand the underlying physics governing the piloting of the ship. Related, the learner may have had previous experience with this game or a similar game and have a general understanding of how the piloting works. This could mean a familiarity with the underlying data representation types, the physics of ship navigation, or specific knowledge of this ship and this geospatial terrain being navigated. In all three of these cases, prior experience with elements related to this specific learning context will have helped develop schemas that can help link past experience with the current need to interpret data visualizations (Hegarty, Carpenter, & Just, 1991; Pinker, 1990; Shah & Hoeffner, 2002).

In addition to the past experiences, individual differences based in more general cognitive abilities can also influence the efficacy of the learning environment

(Gilbert, 2005; Quaiser-Pohl, Geiser, & Lehmann, 2006; Shah & Hoeffner, 2002). These cognitive abilities—influenced by both environmental and genetic factors—include factors such as spatial visualization and metacognitive ability. While it is very difficult to unravel the cause and effect relationship between gaming experience and factors such as mental rotation ability (e.g., Quaiser-Pohl et al., 2006), it is logical that individuals that are good at the skills necessary to perform well in gaming environments also play them more and are more successful at the tasks the games require. The relationship between data visualization and some of these cognitive abilities is a bit different. While gaming is still, by and large, a voluntary activity that has great appeal for many younger learners, data visualization is typically a mandatory school activity that younger students typically don't engage in voluntarily. This means that you have students with a wide range abilities all compelled to some degree to complete tasks that they may or may not have a predilection in which to do well. More scaffolding is required that accommodates a range of abilities and helps equalize the chances of success and, therefore, helps develop the schemas of more novice data visualizers.

Bringing gaming and data visualization together in a single environment now has some interesting implications when looking at experience and ability and their intersection with learner preference and motivation (Mayer & Massa, 2003). Expertise in either area provides the opportunity to tap existing schemas to help solve tasks in these environments quicker and with less mental effort (Larkin & Simon, 1987; Pinker, 1990). While the schema a gamer develops is not the same as the schema experienced data visualizers develop, there is likely to be a large overlapping common basis in visuospatial abilities. Similarly, would putting data visualization tasks in a gaming context provide heightened engagement and motivation to tackle data visualization problems and thus help develop both schemas? On the other hand, if a learner has a weak gaming schema to begin with, does placing the data visualization task in this environment create an additional layer of difficulty in scaffolding a weak data visualization schema?

Cognitive load theory is one way to understand the important learning implications for bringing together innate and learned abilities and the motivation to apply them in this environment (Paas, Renkl, & Sweller, 2003; Sweller, Merrienboer, & Paas, 1998). In particular, how do many of the factors discussed previously come together to influence load on working memory and the cognitive capacity to transform the unfolding experience in the gaming environment into productive long-term schemas. The inherent difficulty of a data-based task within a gaming environment will interact with the abilities of the learner to define the intrinsic cognitive load on the learner. Similarly, the quality of the design of the gaming environment and the embedded data visualization elements will determine how well innate perceptual abilities have been leveraged to keep extraneous cognitive load to a minimum. The motivating and engaging aspects of the data-based tasks being undertaken in the game will determine, in part, the willingness of the learner to expend germane cognitive load to build more robust schemas of the game environment, the types of data visualizations being used, and the larger concepts underlying the immediate tasks.

FUTURE WORK

The world of business and research has increasingly come to depend on generating and interpreting large data sets in order to conduct their work. Accordingly, it follows that there are increasing demands to evolve K-16 instruction to include the development of these abilities (PTCS, 2005; Wiebe & Grable, 2006). To date, much of the research in data visualization has been on understanding the cognitive basis of and the development of tools for use in graduate and post-graduate business and research (Card et al., 1999; Marchionini, 1995). While there has been interesting and innovative work in adopting these professional tools for use in the classroom (Friedman & diSessa, 1999; Gordin et al., 1996), the integration of gaming and data visualization provides an opportunity for a radical break from traditional approaches to bringing data visualization into the classroom and introduce approaches that have neither the "look" nor the "feel" of traditional data visualization tasks but, that at the same time, clearly address the development of key 21st Century data-based decision-making skills.

Future research can go in a number of interesting directions. To begin with, continued development of a theoretical framework for gaming in education should be brought together with the fairly mature field of perception. The challenge will be to bring research that has largely been conducted in decontexualized experimental lab settings into instructional gaming contexts. Similarly, the growing literature from the learning sciences about individual differences and their impact on learning can also be brought together with gaming theory. Clearly a key area here is the growing influence in the research literature of affective dimensions of learning with research on the cognitive and perceptual dimensions. Iterative design experiments offer the opportunity to rigorously develop data visualization activities in gaming environments and then field test them in instructional setting to better understand their impact on learning. Approaches such as this can help unlock the potential for gaming in instruction.

ACKNOWLEDGEMENTS

This work was supported by a grant from the NC GlaxoSmithKline Foundation and from NSF grants DUE/CCLI #9950405 and #0231086 and ESI/IMD #0137811.

REFERENCES

Bertin, J. (1981). *Graphics and graphic information processing*. NY: Walter de Gruyter.
Bertin, J. (1983). *Semiology of graphics: Diagrams networks maps* (W. J. Berg, Trans.). Madison, WI: University of Wisconsin Press.
Bertoline, G. R., & Wiebe, E. N. (2005). *Fundamentals of graphics communication* (5th ed.). New York, NY: McGraw-Hill.
Brown, J. R., Earnshaw, R., Jern, M., & Vince, J. (1995). *Visualization: Using computer graphics to explore data and present information*. NY: Wiley.
Card, S. K., Mackinlay, J. D., & Shneiderman., B. (Eds.). (1999). *Readings in information visualization : Using vision to think*. San Francisco, CA: Morgan Kaufmann.
Cleveland, W. S. (1985). *The elements of graphing data*. Monterey, CA: Wadsworth.

Cleveland, W. S., & McGill, R. (1985). Graphical Perception and Graphical Methods for Analyzing Scientific Data. *Science, 229*, 828-833.

Cunningham, S., Brown, J., & McGrath, M. (1990). Visualization in science and engineering education. In G. M. Nielson & et al (eds.), *Visualization in scientific computing* (pp. 48-57). Washington: IEEE Computer Society Press.

Friedman, J. S., & diSessa, A. A. (1999). What students should know about technology: The case of scientific visualization. *Journal of Science Education and Technology, 8*(3), 175-195.

Gilbert, J. K. (2005). Visualization: A metacognitive skill in science and science education. In J. K. Gilbert (Ed.), *Visualization in science education* (pp. 9-27). Amsterdam: Springer.

Gogel, W. C. (1978). The adjacency principle in visual perception. *Scientific American, 238*(5), 126-139.

Gordin, D. N., Edelson, D. C., & Gomez, L. M. (1996). Scientific visualization as an interpretive and expressive medium. In Edelson & Domeshek (Eds.), *Proceedings of the Second International Conference on the Learning Sciences* (pp. 409-414). Charlottesville, VA: AACE.

Hegarty, M. (2004). Dynamic visualizations and learning: Getting to the difficult questions. *Learning and Instruction, 14*(3), 343-351.

Hegarty, M., Carpenter, P. A., & Just, M. A. (1991). Diagrams in the comprehension of scientific text. In R. Barr, M. L. Kamil, P. B. Mosenthal & P. D. Pearson (Eds.), *Handbook of reading research* (Vol. 2, pp. 641–668). New York: Longman.

Kafai, Y. B. (2006). Playing and making games for learning: Instructionist and Constructionist perspectives for game studies. *Games and Culture, 1*(1), 36-40.

Kafai, Y. B., Franke, M. L., Ching, C. C., & Shih, J. C. (1998). Game design as an interactive learning environment for fostering students' and teachers' mathematical inquiry. *International Journal of Computers for Mathematical Learning, 3*(149-184), 149-184.

Kaiser, M. K., & Proffitt, D. R. (1989). Perceptual issues in scientific visualization. In SPIE (Ed.), *Three-dimensional visualization and display technologies* (Vol. 1083, pp. 205-211).

Larkin, J. H., & Simon, H. A. (1987). Why a diagram is (sometimes) worth ten thousand words. *Cognitive Science BF311 .C552, 11*, 65-99.

Livingston, L., A., Sandals, L. H., & Vickers, J. N. (1992). Monitoring the effect of color on performance in an instructional gaming environment through an analysis of eye movement behaviors. *Journal of research on computing in education, 25*(2), 233-242.

MacEachren, A. M. (1995). *How maps work: Representation, visualization, and design.* New York: Guilford Press.

Marchionini, G. (1995). *Information seeking in electronic environments.* Cambridge, UK: Cambridge University Press.

Mayer, R. E., & Massa, L. J. (2003). Three facets of visual and verbal learners: Cognitive ability, cognitive style, and learning preference. *Journal of Educational Psychology, 95*(4), 833-846.

McCormick, B. H., Defanti, T. A., & Brown, M. D. (1987). Visualization in scientific computing. *(ACM) Computer Graphics, 21*(6).

Mirel, B. (1998). Visualization for data exploration and analysis: A critical review of usability research. *Technical communication, 45*(4), 491-509.

Morse, A. (1979). Some principles for the effective display of data. *(ACM) Computer Graphics, 13*(2), 94-101.

Paas, F., Renkl, A., & Sweller, J. (2003). Cognitive load theory and instructional design: Recent developments. *Educational Psychologist, 38*(1), 1-4.

Pinker, S. (1990). A theory of graph comprehension. In R. Friedle (Ed.), *Artificial intellegence and the future of testing* (pp. 73-126). Norwood, NJ: Ablex.

PTCS, Partnership for 21st Century Skills. (2005). Learning for the 21st Century. Retrieved March, 2006, from http://www.21stcenturyskills.org/images/stories/otherdocs/P21_Report.pdf

Quaiser-Pohl, C., Geiser, C., & Lehmann, W. (2006). The relationship between computer-game preference, gender, and mental-rotation ability. *Personality and Individual Differences, 40*(3), 609-619.

Shah, P., Freedman, E. G., & Vekiri, I. (2005). The comprehension of quantitative information in graphical displays. In P. Shah & A. Miyake (Eds.), *The Cambridge handbook of visuospatial thinking* (pp. 426-476). Cambridge, UK: Cambridge University Press.

Shah, P., & Hoeffner, J. (2002). Review of graph comprehension research: Implications for instruction. *Educational Psychology Review, 14*(1), 47-69.

Shneiderman, B. (1998). *Designing the user interface: Strategies for effective human-computer interaction* (3rd ed.). Reading, MA: Addison-Wesley.

Sweller, J., Merrienboer, J. J. G. v., & Paas, F. G. W. C. (1998). Cognitive architecture and instructional design. *Educational Psychology Review, 10*, 251-296.

Truckenbrod, J. R. (1981). Effective use of color in computer graphics. *(ACM) Computer Graphics, 15*(3), 83-90.

Tufte, E. R. (1983). *The visual display of quantitative information.* Cheshire, CT: Graphics Press.

Wiebe, E. N. (1992). Scientific visualization: An experimental introductory course for scientific and engineering students. *Engineering Design Graphics Journal, 56*(1), 39-44.

Wiebe, E. N., Clark, A. C., & Hasse, E. V. (2001). Scientific visualization: Linking science and technology education through graphic communications. *Journal of Design and Technology Education, 6*(1), 40-47.

Wiebe, E. N., & Grable, L. L. (2006, November). *21st century teaching and learning in middle school science.* Paper presented at the NC Science Teachers Association Annual Meeting, Greensboro, NC.

Xing, J. (2006). *Color and visual factors in ATC displays* (Final Report No. DOT/FAA/AM-06/15). Oklahoma City, OK: Civil Aerospace Medical Institute, Federal Aviation Administration.

Eric N. Wiebe
North Carolina State University

MICHELLE COOK

CHAPTER 6

Problem-Based Learning as the Backbone for Educational Game Design

INTRODUCTION

Video games in the classroom have the potential to enhance learning, yet few guidelines exist for creating these virtual environments (Pedersen, Lui, & Williams, 2002). Many of the games that have made their way into the classroom follow the drill-and-practice model, emphasizing rote memorization and failing to capture the interest of students (Squire & Jenkins, 2003). How can we harness this medium to enhance science education with pedagogically sound yet entertaining games? When considering how to design these learning environments, it becomes evident that natural ties exist between video game creation and problem-based learning. Problem-based learning is an instructional model whereby learning results from students' efforts to solve a complex problem. This chapter will provide an overview of problem-based learning. The foundations of problem-based learning will be presented, as well as the stages involved in this instructional approach. In addition, the benefits of problem-based learning will be introduced, with emphasis on the cognitive and affective role of this model in the classroom. Finally, several guidelines for creating virtual problem-based learning environments will be presented.

WHAT IS PROBLEM-BASED LEARNING?

Problem-based learning has its origins in medical education, but is now used in a wide range of disciplines at a variety of educational levels. It is an instructional approach where students are confronted with a problem and challenged to work towards a solution. The problem is complex and ill-structured, and does not provide enough information for a simple resolution. The presentation of fragmented information, along with the students' assumption of roles that provide a connection to the situation, motivates learners through the problem-solving process. In order to solve the problem, students will have to engage in a variety of activities such as observing, gathering information, forming hypotheses, conducting experiments, and analysing data. As students tackle these activities, they begin to realize that there is no simple or fixed solution to the problem and that their task will be to use the information they have collected to justify the best possible solution.

L.A. Annetta (ed.), Serious Educational Games: From Theory to Practice, 57–63.

The Foundations of Problem-Based Learning

Teachers recognize the importance of teaching students to work through problem situations by identifying the key issues, gathering information, and developing a viable solution. However, most practitioners are familiar with traditional teaching models in which students first learn the content material through direct instruction before they are given the opportunity to apply it in structured learning situations, problem sets, or test-items. In this model, the teacher teaches, the student learns, and then the student can apply what s/he has learned (Torp & Sage 1998). This model assumes that applying knowledge is a simple process, not dependent on the context in which the knowledge was learned, and that students will recognize when to apply this knowledge (Bridges & Hallinger, 1995).

Problem-based learning follows a different paradigm (learner-centred) and is more in line with the current movement to reform science education (American Association for the Advancement of Science, 1993; National Research Council, 1996). In problem-based learning, the learning experience imparts knowledge to be used rather than facts to be acquired (Bell, Bareiss, & Beckwith, 1993). Students are confronted with a situation where they assume the role of a stakeholder and through investigation, learn whatever is necessary to arrive at a justifiable solution. Because the task is authentic and their engagement with it has been sustained, students appreciate the utility of the knowledge they are learning and can recognize when this knowledge is applicable (Bransford et al., 1990). Since the new knowledge is encoded in a context that mirrors how it will subsequently be used, it increases the chance that the student will remember and apply what is stored in memory (Barab et al., 2001).

The fundamental ideas underlying problem-based learning are directly related to constructivist ideas of teaching and learning (Pearson, 2006). Learning is an active process requiring mental construction on the part of the learner. Problem-based learning activates prior knowledge and facilitates learning by encouraging students to incorporate new knowledge with their existing knowledge. With this instructional method, learners experience a cognitive conflict, when their way of thinking does not produce what is expected (Savery & Duffy, 1995). According the Piaget, this conflict or perturbation, leads to accommodation and adaptation (Koschmann et al., 1994). The problem-solving process encourages the learner to continually modify and appraise their understanding and guides them to a new sense of equilibrium.

Also at the heart of problem-based learning is the idea that learning is a social process. Cognitive change often occurs as a result of interaction with other students who may hold different understandings (von Glasersfeld, 1989). Since these social interactions with peers may challenge and refine a student's current views, problem-based learning provides students with an opportunity to articulate new knowledge (Koschmann et al., 1994). Social negotiation also occurs when students interact with the teacher. A teacher's role in this process becomes guiding students as they direct their own learning process. A teacher facilitates learning through clarifying, questioning, coaching, modelling, challenging student thinking, encouraging collaboration, monitoring student thinking and dispositions, and providing feedback (Torp & Sage, 1998).

The Stages of Problem-Based Learning

In problem-based learning, learning is framed by the context of the problem scenario. Therefore, in the first step, students are presented with the problem. Students assume a role and become stakeholders to promote engagement in the learning experience (Koszalka, Grabowski, & Younghoon, 2002). At this stage, students identify the problem, obtain clarification about the problem, and identify their central task. Next, students are asked to develop a plan of study. They must identify what they know about the problem, what they need to know to solve the problem, and their ideas for what actions they might need to take. This step helps access the students' prior knowledge and provides focus to the investigation (Goodnough & Cashion, 2006).

Once students have defined the problem and identified the steps they need to take to solve it, they begin the process of collecting and sharing information. Gathering information may involve speaking with experts in the field, researching primary sources, conducting experiments, participating in hands-on activities, using a simulation, or taking a field trip. After analysing the evidence they have collected, students are asked to generate possible solutions to the problem and determine the best-fit solution. During this step, peers work to help each other refine their understandings as they discuss the merits of each solution plan. Finally, students are asked to share their solutions through an authentic performance assessment (Koszalka, Grabowski, & Younghoon, 2002). Throughout the stages, teachers must embed periodic assessments to gauge student learning and provide information as to how to best facilitate the process. Assessment strategies include concept maps, problem logs, journals, presentations, posters, proposals, interviews, articles, and debates.

BENEFITS OF PROBLEM-BASED LEARNING

Numerous benefits result from problem-based learning. First, students gain enhanced problem-solving abilities (Samsonov, Pedersen, & Hill, 2006). Since problem-based learning promotes critical thinking, students develop a deeper understanding of the knowledge domain as compared with traditional learning (Akinoglu & Tandogan, 2007; Krynock & Robb, 1996). As a result, students have better long-term knowledge retention and are better able to transfer their learning to solve new problems (Lui et al., 2006). Problem-based learning also engages students in a holistic learning experience. Not only do students learn more about the discipline of primary interest, but they also learn how that discipline relates to other knowledge domains (Torp & Sage, 1998).

In addition, students experience high levels of intrinsic motivation resulting from being a stakeholder in an interesting, real-world problem and having more opportunities to interact with their peers (Albanese & Mitchell 1993; Vernon &

Blake, 1993). Students are motivated to invest the cognitive effort required to gather information and develop the skills needed to justify a solution. Without this "willing cognition," students may neglect to recognize the intricacies of the problem, fail to fully explore the learning resources, and develop non-viable solutions (Pedersen, Lui, & Williams, 2006). Students engaged in problem-based learning also become more effective at self-regulating their learning. In essence, students learn how to learn. (Barab et al., 2001)

GUIDELINES FOR DESIGNING VIRTUAL PROBLEM-BASED LEARNING ENVIRONMENTS

While there are numerous benefits to the approach, the literature indicates that implementing problem-based learning can be challenging. However, technology creates "new opportunities for curriculum and instruction by bringing in real-world problems into the classroom for students to explore and solve" (Bransford, Brown, & Cocking, 2000, p. 195). The additional support from computer-based tools may enhance the delivery and extend the benefits of this instructional strategy to a wider range of audiences (Lui et al., 2006), yet few guidelines exist for creating these virtual environments. The following insights are intended to help the guide the design of these virtual problem-based learning environments.

Consider the Learners and the Curriculum

Designers must first consider student learning characteristics and interests. For the particular educational level they are targeting, it is important to take into account the knowledge, skills, and dispositions students possess. While it is essential that the game be engaging and fun, the designer must use this knowledge of student characteristics to find a balance between making the game challenging yet not too simple. The game should target the outer limits of student abilities (Squire & Jenkins, 2003). In addition, game designers must also consider the curriculum. What conceptual, skill-based, and dispositional outcomes are valued at that particular educational level? To ensure the game addresses the targeted objectives, designers can map out problem ideas and connections after the learning environment has been conceptualised (Torp & Sage, 1998).

Develop an Engaging and Complex Problem

The problem scenario needs to hook students. Often times, this involves creating a role for students to assume so that they feel connected to the problem and able to impact change. This is what Shaffer (2004) called Epistemic Games. Students can be environmental scientists, epidemiologists, genetic counsellors, or forensic scientists; however in some instances, the most appropriate role may be that of a student. Problem situations can emerge from significant concepts in the curriculum, current events, or seeds of interest (Koszalka, Grabowski, & Younghoon, 2002). And although students respond positively to authentic learning situations, problems do not have to be real-world if they spark student interest (Pedersen, Lui, & Williams, 2002).

Problem scenarios must also be complex. Students should recognize that the problem does not provide them with all of the information needed. If students are not challenged by the problem, they may assume there is a single, obvious solution and be reluctant to invest effort into the problem. On the other hand, the complexity of the problem needs to be balanced with manageability. Students must not get frustrated or feel like the problem is too difficult to be solved. They must also feel like the problem can be solved in the time allotted. This balance between presenting complex yet manageable problems is a secret video game designers in the entertainment industry have known for years—games should be hard enough to be just doable (Squire & Jenkins, 2003).

Provide an Adequate Number of Resources

Students need to seek out large amounts of information in problem-based learning. Students should be provided access to these informational resources within the virtual environment. Game designers should provide students with more resources than are necessary to solve the problem (without suggesting the usefulness of the resources) so that students begin to discriminate between useful and non-useful information (Pedersen, Lui, & Williams, 2002). In addition, the information should be provided in various formats (experimental data, expert opinion, textbook information, etc.); however, regardless of the format, resources should be designed as to not overwhelm the students or provide too much structure.

Include Many Smaller Problems in the Learning Environment

As students are engaged in the learning experiences, they should encounter smaller complexities that need to be pursued in order to solve the larger problem. For example, students may have to perform an experiment and interpret data, interview an expert, conduct an interview, or participate in a field study in order to move forward in the process (Barab et al., 2005). This allows students to practice multiple problem-solving strategies, encourages them to reflect on the effectiveness of these strategies, provides them with opportunities for discussion and feedback (Pedersen, Lui, & Williams, 2002).

Create the Need for Student Collaboration

While student collaboration is not always essential in problem-based learning, it has two very important benefits. Interaction with peers has a positive effect on motivation and may help students to reflect on and refine their own ideas (Pederson, 2003). Designers can build this interaction into games by creating multi-user environments where students must collaborate to solve the problem. In these games, students are unable to handle the complexity of the problem situation individually and are forced work together to investigate, weigh evidence, synthesize information, and draw conclusions (Squire & Jenkins, 2003). Designers can even take this idea a step further by creating multiple roles for students to play. For example, in a beach erosion problem, students could assume different roles, such as homeowners, marine scientists, or tourism representatives.

Create Opportunities to Facilitate Learning

An important part of the problem-based learning process is the role the teacher plays as a cognitive coach. Game designers must ensure that this type of pedagogical support is included in the virtual environment. Games can include modelling (when an expert demonstrates the problem-solving process), coaching (when suggestions are made on student performance at appropriate times), and scaffolding (when tools are provided to decrease the complexity of the task) (Bell, Bareiss, & Beckwith, 1993). In addition to computer-based support, games designers must consider how teachers can interact with students playing the game. Teacher support will still be necessary to clarify questions, push students to articulate their thinking, assess learning, and promote collaboration (Torp & Sage, 1998).

Learning Through Failure

Keeping in mind self-efficacy and self-esteem, one might argue that learning through failure could be detrimental. When designing an educational video game it is crucial to consider how adults learn and how we might train our students for success through failure. Henry Petroski describes how learning from one's own mistakes can be beneficial and gives explicit examples from packaging Advil to the Space Shuttle. These are the real-world examples that one might begin to formulate problem based learning activities for game design.

REFERENCES

Akinoglu, O., & Tandogan, R.O. (2007). The effects of problem-based active learning in science education on students' academic achievement, attitude, and concept learning. *Eurasia Journal of Mathematics, Science, and Technology Education, 3*(1), 71-81.

Albanese, M.A., & Mitchell, S. (1993). Problem-based learning: A review of literature on its outcomes and implementation issues. *Academic Medicine, 68*(1), 52-81.

American Association for the Advancement of Science. (1993). *Benchmarks for scientific literacy.* New York, NY: Oxford University Press.

Barab, S.A., Hay, K.E., Barnett, M., & Squire, K. (2001). Constructing virtual worlds: Tracing the historical development of learner practices. *Cognition and Instruction, 19*(1), 47-94.

Barab, S., Thomas, M., Dodge, T., Carteaux, R., & Tuzum, H. (2005). Making learning fun: Quest Atlantis, a game without guns. *Educational Technology Research & Development, 53*(1), 86-107.

Bell, B., Bareiss, R., & Beckwith, R. (1993). Sickle cell counselor: A prototype goal-based scenario for instruction in a museum environment. *The Journal of the Learning Sciences, 3*(4), 347-386.

Bransford, J.D., Brown, A.L., & Cocking, R.R. (Eds.). (2000). *How people learn: Brain, mind, experience and school.* Washington, DC: National Academy Press.

Bransford, J.D, Sherwood, R.D., Hasselbring, T.S., Kinzer, C.K., & Williams, S.M. (1990). Anchored instruction: Why we need it and how technology can help. In R. Spiro & D. Nix (eds.) *Cognition, education, and multimedia: Exploring ideas in high technology* (pp. 115-141). Hillsdale, NJ: Lawrence Erlbaum Associates, Inc.

Bridges, E.M., & Hallinger, P. (1995). *Implementing problem-based learning in leadership development.* Eugene, OR: ERIC Clearinghouse on Educational Management.

Goodnough, K., & Cashion, M. (2006) Exploring problem-based learning in context of high school science: Design and implementation issues. *School Science and Mathematics, 106*(7), 280-295.

Koschmann, T.D., Myers, A.C., Feltovich, P.J., & Barrows, H.S. (1994). Using technology to assist in realizing effective learning and instruction: A principled approach to the use of computers in collaborative learning. *The Journal of the Learning Sciences, 3*(3), 227-264.

Koszalka, T.A., Grabowski, B., & Younghoon, K. (2002). *Designing web-based science lesson plans that use problem-based learning to inspire middle school kids: KaAMS (Kids as Airborne Mission Scientists).* Paper presented at the annual meeting of the American Educational Research Association, New Orleans, LA.

Krynock, K.B., & Robb, L. (Fall 1996). Is problem-based learning a problem for your curriculum? *Illinois School Research and Development Journal, 33*(1), 21-24.

Lui, M., Hsieh, P., Cho, Y., & Schallert, D.L. (2006). Middle school students' self-efficacy, attitudes, and achievement in a computer-enhanced problem-based learning environment. *Journal of Interactive Learning Research, 17*(3), 255-242.

National Research Council. (1996). *National science education standards.* Washington, DC: National Academy Press.

Pearson, J. (2006). Investigating ICT using problem-based learning in face-to-face and online learning environments. *Computers & Education, 47*(1), 56-73.

Pedersen, S. (2003). Motivational orientation in a problem-based learning environment. *Journal of Interactive Learning Research, 14*(1), 51-77.

Pedersen, S., Lui, M., & Williams, D. (2002). Alien Rescue: Designing for student-centered learning. *Educational Technology, 42*(5), 11-14.

Samsonov, P., Pedersen, S., & Hill, C.L. (2006) Using problem-based learning software with at-risk students: A case study. *Computers in the Schools, 23*(1/2), 111-124.

Savery, J.R., & Duffy, T.M. (1995). Problem-based learning: An instructional model and its constructivist framework. *Educational Technology, 35*(5), 31-35.

Shaffer, D. W., Squire, K., Halverson, R., Gee, J. P. (2004). "Video Games and the Future of Learning." Madison, WI: University of Wisconsin-Madison and Academic Advanced Distributed Learning Co-Laboratory.

Squire, K., & Jenkins, H. (2003). Harnessing the power of games in education. *Insight, 3*(1), 5-33.

Torp, L., & Sage, S. (1998). *Problems as possibilities: Problem-based learning for K-12 education.* Alexandria, VA: Association for Supervision and Curriculum Development.

Vernon, D., & Blake, R. (1993). Does problem-based learning work? A meta-analysis of evaluative research. *Academic Medicine, 7*(1), 550-563.

von Glasersfeld, E. (1989). Cognition, construction of knowledge, and teaching. *Synthese, 80*, 121-140.

Michelle Cook
Teacher Education, Clemson University

WALTER ROTENBERRY

CHAPTER 7

From the Problem to the Story to the Storyboard

INTRODUCTION

This chapter discusses the basics of creating the back-story and subsequential storyboard as part of the preproduction process of game development. The back-story is often considered the "why" behind the game. The back-story is sometimes employed to lend the main story depth. It may include the history of characters, objects, countries, or other elements of the main story. Its purpose is usually to reveal in part or in full, how the main narrative will unfold. From a good story, a story board must be integrated to complete the preproduction process. Storyboards are like a large comic strip of the entire game or of some section of the game. They are produced beforehand to help designers, producers, and possibly clients visualize the scenes. Storyboards can also be used to find potential problems before they occur and often include arrows or instructions that indicate the game flow. This chapter will provide the back-story elements with concrete examples from popular commercial games.

THE BACK STORY

Today's video games align closely with the popular culture movies. The process starts with a story and evolves into an entertaining, engaging product. The **back-story** is the history behind the situation existing at the start of the main story. In education, it is the problem in a problem-based learning scenario (see Chapter 2 of this book). Back-stories can be revealed in full but in most video games it is typically somewhat brief. Most players are not patient enough to watch a five or ten minute text-based or cinematic introduction before playing a new game. They want to play now! This is just as true with Serious Games, so teaching history, for example, may need to be as much part of the game as it is the back-story.

Back-stories are often chronological as the main narrative unfolds, however this is not required. Sometimes a player will learn about the history as he journeys through the game. In other cases, back-stories are not required at all. In games like Solitaire, there is no additional information needed to enjoy playing. Back-stories are especially useful when a game places the player in unfamiliar situations, such as when students learning a new subject. The use of both verbal and nonverbal

L.A. Annetta (ed.), Serious Educational Games: From Theory to Practice, 65–74.

elements and visual effects are easy and effective tools that can help to reduce the length of the back-story.

Serious Game designer must ask: Do we need a back-story? This may depend on the genre that is chosen for the learning experience. Games like Pong have no stories at all, in fact, stories as part of video games did not come into fashion until the mid 1980's. Adventure and role-playing games began to focus on more on the adventures of the characters-consequently taking on a third-person point of view. Today we see stories and back-stories in many of the top selling video games and in a modern educational game having a frame of reference for the student as a starting point can be critical.

Story Elements

Elements of a good back-story may include the setting, the characters, the plot and conflict. The setting is the game world and refers to the time and place in which the story is set. The setting provides the main backdrop for the story and often creates the overall tone for the game.
Example:

> **Gears of War** takes place on *Sera*, a planet inhabited by humans, who have warred over a phosphorescent, low-viscosity fluid known as "Imulsion." Over several decades the "Pendulum Wars" took place between various human countries, and ended with the *Coalition of Ordered Governments* (COG) taking control of the planet. However, the War quickly came to an end on "Emergence Day," when a ravenous force known as the *Locust Horde* burst from underneath major human cities using a network of underground tunnels. The Coalition, unable to defend against the sudden attack, was routed, and the Locust Horde took control of the majority of Sera's urban, military, and manufacturing centers within 24 hours. The COG ordered any survivors that could make it to *Jacinto Plateau*, a safe haven from Locust underground attacks, and then used orbital laser weapons in a scorched earth strategy to deny the Locust Horde its gains. The human survivors that could not make it became known as the "Stranded" and had to survive on their own. In the fourteen years since "Emergence Day", the Locust continued to attack the fortified Jacinto Plateau and have forced the COG to turn to the infirm, the young, and the condemned to replace their dwindling numbers.

The character can include people, robots, aliens or almost any object controlled by the player. Full character development in a game is difficult and is often left to simply giving descriptive names, revealing how a character/team gained their superpowers, or the circumstances under which they became superheroes or super-villains. More recently characters are starting to become more developed as the graphics have increased in quality to give a better impression of the character.
Example:

Marcus Fenix in *Gears of War*. Fenix is first introduced into *Gears of War* as a <u>prison inmate</u>. Once a talented soldier, Fenix was prosecuted for abandoning his military post in order to rescue his father and he is sentenced to serve forty years in prison for his desertion. Years after the events, Fenix's prison is attacked by Locust forces. Jay Hawkins, concept artist for *Gears of War*, says of Marcus Fenix " … is Clint Eastwood mixed with a Mack Truck, all wrapped up in body armor."

The back-story plot is generally short and may start with an introductory section where the player first meets the character he will control for the rest of the game. Example:

In *Gears of War* the plot begins fourteen years after Emergence Day when <u>Marcus Fenix</u> is reinstated into the military after spending years in prison. <u>Dominic Santiago</u>, successfully extracts him from the prison, and takes him to meet Delta Squadron. The group seeks to obtain the "resonator", a device that will allow them to map the Locust Tunnel, and later deploy the "Lightmass Bomb", which will destroy the heart of the Locust forces.

The conflict is the central struggle between objects controlled by the player and those controlled by the opponents often alluded to in the back-story. Example:

In *Gears of War,* as told by <u>Jonathan Miller</u> of IGN, the underground monsters have superhuman size and strength, with filthy complexions that could rival the ugliest of teens, the Locust are fearsome creatures. And on a sunny Sera afternoon, the Locusts emerged to battle or conflict with the humans.

A story creator may also create portions of a back-story or even an entire back-story that is solely for his or her own use in writing the main story. It may never be revealed in the main story. In *Gears of War* the back-story is not in the game. You have to read the game manual to learn about it. This is yet another way of communicating the backstory (along with cinematic events, on-screen text, and/or animated characters with audio overlay). Why? Because people want to play the game! After they become engrossed they might choose to go back and read the story to gain a better understanding.

THE ELDER SCROLLS

<u>The Elder Scrolls</u> is a <u>role-playing game</u> series <u>developed</u> by <u>Bethesda Softworks</u>® which features a vast and complex back-story. This is personal history of the characters in the game – the story of their lives and/or ancestors' lives. Many varying and contradictory accounts of back-stories in the games exist in the virtual game world of Tamriel - the accidental confusion, mythologisation and ideological appropriation of histories in the series gives the games a very rich and compelling atmosphere of authenticity. It also maintains the player's interest by allowing them

to try and piece together the 'true' version of events. Some events, however, such as the <u>War of the Second House</u>, were deliberately not given definitive 'true' versions by the designers, so as to enhance the aforementioned atmosphere.

The Elder Scrolls places great emphasis on the idea of the dualism and equality of opposites. This dualism is not the famous dualism of good and evil, but more closely resembles a fusion of Eastern and pre-<u>Christian</u> Western beliefs on the subject, being the duality of order and chaos. According to *Elder Scrolls Lore*, the concepts of order and chaos can be translated collectively into everything. These notions might be more exactly approximated using the words **stasis** (unchanging continuity) and **force** (unknowable energy). Almost all Tamrielic religions strongly feature the idea that the world was created through an *intermingling* of these two things, some saying that **time** is a synthesis of continuity and alteration, and most religious creation-theories deal with one or more mythological characters representing these absolutes either procreating or engaging in combat (*or both, as the case may be*). The thought experiment of the <u>irresistible force</u> is often invoked, and much of the Elder Scrolls <u>theosophical</u> lore is devoted to developing and examining hypotheses as to how such a thought experiment might actually play out on all levels, were it <u>metaphysically</u> possible.

INTEGRATING THE MAIN STORY WITH THE BACKSTORY

Stories have probably been shared in every culture and in every land as a means of <u>entertainment</u>, education, preservation of culture, and to instill knowledge. Crucial elements of storytelling include the same elements as the backstory such as plot and characters but are much more developed. Stories are still frequently used to teach, explain, and entertain. Less frequently, but occasionally with major consequences, they have been used to mislead.

Technology has changed the tools available to storytellers. The earliest forms of storytelling are thought to be primarily oral combined with gestures and expressions. Rudimentary drawings, such as can be seen in the artwork scratched onto the walls of caves, may also have been early forms of storytelling. With the invention of <u>writing</u>, stories were recorded, transcribed and shared over wide regions of the world. Stories have been carved, scratched, painted into and onto just about everything from bones to paper to silk. Today a vast entertainment industry has been built upon a foundation of sophisticated multimedia storytelling in a new arena, video games.

An example of a simple story:

A young Navy guy knowing that he has an inspection in the morning, takes all his white uniforms to the laundry. He loads the machine and goes on about his business. While he is gone, another guy drops a new red tee shirt into the machine. The next morning at inspection you see a sea of white uniforms on the deck of a large ship and one lone guy wearing pink.

How a back-story might change your impression of this story:

The young guy washing his uniforms was a bodybuilding brute that had beaten and robbed the little 98lb. weakling with the red tee shirt the day before.

Or:

The young new guy while washing his uniforms was ordered to clean deck by the guy with the red shirt – who was supposed to clean the deck. The new guy refused; he had his own work to do. The bully with the red shirt was trying to intimidate the new guy and show him who rules the ship.

Here the point in the story can be short and the back-story can give important details that can change the impression of the story.

One popular technique to aid in story development and expressing story themes is to collaborate with an artistic colleague on a storyboard.

Storyboards are graphic organizers such as a series of <u>illustrations</u> or <u>images</u> displayed in sequence to present and describe <u>interactive</u> events as well as <u>motion</u>. A newspaper comic strip is an example. An interactive media storyboard may be used for the design of a video game or simulation and aids in telling the story and how the motion flows. Storyboards allow the user to experiment with changes in the storyline to evoke stronger reaction or interest. Storyboards also aid in the process of visual thinking and planning which allows a group of people to brainstorm together, placing their ideas on storyboards, then arranging the storyboards on a wall. This can foster more ideas and generates consensus inside the group.

An example storyboard from the sailor narrative

First, break it down into four scenes. Scene one: the guy puts his clothes in the washer. Scene two: the guy walks away. Scene three: another guy has the lid of the machine open and is holding a red tee shirt above it. Scene four: the first guy is standing in pink among all the other guys in white. It is necessary to draw an arrow leading from scene one to scene four showing the flow of the storyboard.

A good Storyboard can contain much more than this. If you can imagine a comic strip, with video game language subtitles and the speech bubbles written as a sound effects panel, (along with any other sounds made in that shot or scene) you are approaching the amount of content required for a good storyboard. In fact, almost every person involved in a video game's production needs to refer to either the script and/or the storyboard at some stage.

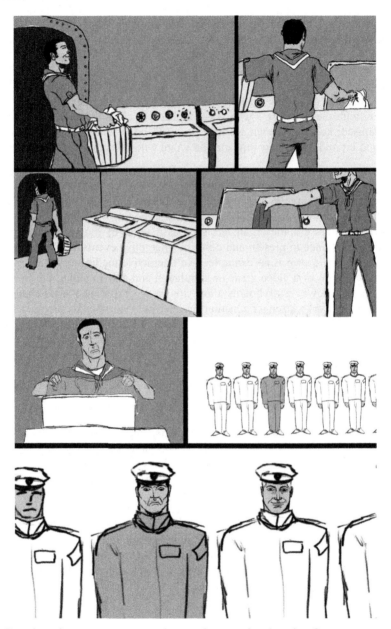

The Storyboard can act as a preview and as a visual script for camera angles, lighting, montage, sound effects, actor arrangement, prop arrangement, and (most importantly) the narrative development and continuity. If a video game production team arrived for work on the first day of a new project, and there was no such thing as a storyboard, the following are just some of the problems that could be expected:

- Because the script would be in written form there would be a danger of misunderstanding the descriptions or video game terms.
- There could be language differences. Pictures are the International story language.
- The Producer would have to have incredible vision to be able to see how the story flowed and if the continuity was correct.

There are actually several types of storyboards, the main one being the Production Storyboard.

1. The Production Storyboard. The example above is similar to a production adapted for student use. Refer to the Conventions section for an explanation of the Shot codes.
2. Conceptual Sheet or Painting. This is a sequence of images. The purpose of this is simply to communicate the visual style of the video game.
3. The Digital or Rush Storyboard is a Production Storyboard that has been compiled using digital images, either tableau-style posed images or actual stills from rehearsals or exploratory shooting. There is Software available for this type of storyboard. The advantage of this type is that non-linear editors can re-arrange the shots or adjust various aspects of the storyboard instantly and this gives the Director wider choice and a problem-solving facility.

WHAT ARE THE MAIN CONVENTIONS?

The film, TV, and adverting industry use variations of these as well. A lot of information is communicated through a storyboard and the industry has created its own language and conventions. This allows producers to make their own shorthand and everyone in the industry should be familiar with the technical terms and the codes used. The following is a brief look at some of the main conventions. Many of these codes and conventions are transferable. That is they hold a similar meaning in another part of the industry.

The story that is told is broken down into narrative elements. These are the Characters, the Setting, the Conflicts, and the Resolution of the story. Most of these elements are detailed in the script but are referred to in the storyboard. The Characters perform the actions required to complete the narrative. In a given setting the story moves from a state of equilibrium to situations that involve conflicts that must be resolved. These add drama and tension to the plot. They also allow for interweaving sub-plots into the main story plot.

Any one story in real time would be tedious and time-consuming. To condense this and inject interest, the plot is broken down further into important events or situations called moments. What follows is an example of storyboarding a longer narrative by moments:

1. EMS arrives on the scene.
2. There is a person lying on the grass.

3. There is a policeman running over.
4. The paramedics lean over the victim.
5. Shots are heard.
6. The paramedics rush the victim to the ambulance as the victim says "help me"
7. Bullets ring past them and hit the policeman.
8. The body slumps.
9. The paramedics rush to help him.

Camera Angles

The industry varies slightly in the exact code headings, however many will be familiar with the following:

- **Establishing or Long Shot (LS)** -generally used to establish a scene's setting or atmosphere. This shot could be employed for events 1 and 2 in the example above.
- **Mid -Shot. (MS)** This shot usually extends (on a person) from the foot to the head. This could be an ideal shot for event 3 (above).
- **Close-up (CU)** traditionally extends from either the waist to the head (MCU) or the shoulder blade to the hair.(CU) A good candidate for the shot for events5 and 8 (above).
- **Big Close Up (BCU)** Always a very tight close-up, usually of the face or a section of the face only. Maximum expression possible. Normally a short shot. Ideal for event 6 (above).
- **High Camera Angle (HCA)** The camera is higher than eye level, looking down -this viewpoint can diminish a subject or give a panorama.
- **Low Camera Angle (LCA)** The camera is lower than eye level looking up. This can make a subject monumental, or the character feel small in a tall environment.

GETTING STARTED

1. Write a Synopsis of the plot (narrative) for the video game.
2. Break up the plot into Moments.
3. Pencil in the scenes and shots. (This can be done with 'stick' figures and along with descriptions)
4. Analyze.

Camera Angle shots are required to enhance a scene. This time, because you have clearer images, look for continuity and theme development. Changes or additions can be referenced. Put it all in order as it will be played in the game. Remember, very few video games are linear. Most allow the player to take different paths. A good storyboard will have a path for each action the player can take.

Here are some tips for an outstanding longer story adapted from Syd Field's book *Screenplay*:

Opening Image: The first image should summarize the entire video game, especially its tone. Often, this is the last thing before submission of the story.

Catalyst: This is the point in the story when the protagonist encounters the problem that will change their life. This is when the detective is assigned to the case, where boy meets girl, and where the comic hero gets fired from his cushy job, forcing him into comic circumstances.

Turning Point 1: The last scene in Act One, Turning Point One is a surprising development that radically changes the protagonist's life, and forces him to confront the opponent.

Pinch 1: A reminder scene at about 3/8 of the way through that brings up the central conflict of the drama, reminding us of the overall conflict.

Midpoint: An important scene in the middle of the script, often a reversal of fortune or revelation that changes the direction of the story.

Pinch 2: Another reminder scene about 5/8 through the script that is somehow linked to Pinch 1 in reminding the gamer about the central conflict.

Turning Point 2: A dramatic reversal that is about confrontation and resolution. Sometimes Turning Point Two is the moment when the hero has had enough and is finally going to face the opponent.

Showdown: The protagonist will confront the main problem of the story and either overcomes it, or comes to a tragic end.

Resolution: The issues of the story are resolved.

Tag: An epilogue, tying up the loose ends of the story, giving the audience closure.

Once you have agreed on the storyboard and put the story in order, it is time to write the story. Writing the story for a video game is much like writing a screenplay. To write a good video game it is important to recognize the style, craft, and structure of video games. One way is by reading the screenplays of popular and successful movies. The time necessary to write a story varies widely upon the writer and the circumstances. Professional writers frequently are called upon to write an hour-long script in less than a week while major scripts have literally taken years of rewrites before they are ready. Most professional writers can complete two to three original works in a year.

CONCLUSION

The engaging nature of today's video games is arguable due to the immersive storylines present in each respective game. For education, one could teach about reading and writing through the backstories found in popular video games. Books were once the main vehicle of communicating rich stories but as technology pervades, new literacies are forming. It is critical that educators embrace these

WALTER ROTENBERRY

technologies and impact student learning through the complex story structures found in video games.

REFERENCES

http://gearsofwar.com/BehindTheScenes/Interview_Jay_Hawkins.htm
http://xbox360.ign.com/articles/744/744356p1.html
http://en.wikipedia.org/wiki/Gears_of_War

Walter Rotenberry
Wake Technical Community College

JAMES MINOGUE

CHAPTER 8

Getting a "Feel" For Serious Games

INTRODUCTION

As humans we commonly (and seemingly effortlessly) use our hands to learn about the world around us as we use sensory information gained through touch to build our understandings of complex objects and events. Relatively recent advances in technology have made the addition of "touch" to computer-generated virtual environments possible. As a result there is a burgeoning research base on haptics but despite such work, touch has emerged as an understudied and perhaps underutilized sensory modality in the creation of computer-mediated instructional programs, including video games. This chapter will take an honest look at the potential impact of haptic technology on the Serious Games movement. More specifically, this section of the book will briefly describe currently available haptic interfaces, outline what is known about the processing of haptic information as it pertains to the complex teaching-learning process, and 'take stock' of where we are in terms of haptically augmented educational games in an attempt to plot a prudent course for future work in this arena.

A BRIEF HISTORY OF HAPTICS

What is Haptics?

Computer technology has provided information to the human senses of sight and hearing as audio and video systems have been perfected over many decades. But relatively recently a surge in computer capability coupled with the desire to create improved ways to connect to computer generated worlds have lead to the development of haptic devices.

The word "haptic" is derived from the Greek terms *haptesthai* which translates to *able to lay hold of* and *haptikos* meaning *able to touch* (Revesz, 1950; Katz, 1989). Current uses of the term most often refer to the study of touch and the human interaction with the external environment via touch. Inherently multidisciplinary, the field of haptics includes work from disciplines such as engineering, psychology, cognitive science, computer science, and to a much lesser extent, educational technology (Minogue & Jones, 2006). Haptic technology has its roots in robotic teleoperation that was developed for work in dangerous nuclear

L.A. Annetta (ed.), Serious Educational Games: From Theory to Practice, 75–83.

environments (Goertz, 1952; Goertz, 1964). In a sense, the teleoperator device is replaced by a computer which allows for the creation of a "virtual" environment (unrestricted by normal physical constraints).

Haptic Feedback

Today, an ever increasing number of research groups are involved in the development, testing, and refinement of haptic interfaces that allow users to "feel" and manipulate three-dimensional (3D) virtual objects (McLaughlin, Hespanha & Sukhatme, 2002; Hatwell, Streri & Gentaz, 2003). These multimodal interfaces can be programmed to provide realistic force feedback (e.g. simulating object compliance, weight, and inertia) and/or tactile feedback (e.g. simulating surface contact geometry, smoothness, slippage, and temperature). By employing physical receptors in the hand and arm that gather sensory information the user attempts to draw conclusions about virtual objects and events (Jacobson, Kitchen, & Golledge, 2000). In essence, current haptic interfaces strive to unite the human haptic and machine haptic subsystems in an optimal way, as depicted in Figure 1.

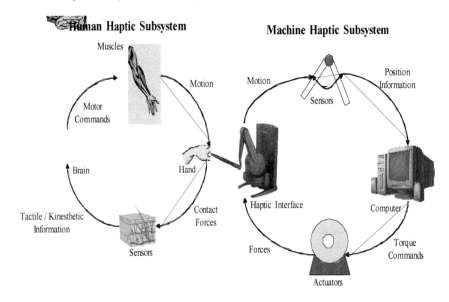

Figure 1. A depiction of a typical haptic interface's subsystems.

However, enabling programmable bi-directional touch interaction with virtual environments is not a trivial task. It involves engineering, computing, and perceptual challenges that include sensing the state of a haptic device, computing haptic collision detection, updating the status of the virtual object(s), as well as computing and displaying the necessary forces and/or torques to the user (De-La-Torre, 2006). To further complicate things, these tasks are best preformed at rates of 1 kHz or higher, at lower rates noticeable visual and haptic feedback mismatches can occur in space and/or time. Such disparities can ultimately undermine the realism of the virtual displays and lead to the gathering of erroneous sensory information.

HAPTIC INTERFACES

Currently available haptic devices vary in sophistication and fidelity. At one end of the spectrum lie vibrating game pads and force-feedback gaming joysticks which offer limited interactivity. These devices churn out rather crude haptic effects usually via open loop feedback and/or predefined feedback signals. At the other end of the continuum reside the sophisticated "laboratory-grade" haptic devices. These apparatuses seamlessly marry complicated software and intricate hardware to provide the user with a high level of interactivity and fine-grained sensory clues. Naturally, the cost of haptic devices mirrors this range in capabilities. The high-end tools used by haptics researchers have been grouped into two broad categories: data gloves and point-probe devices (Burdea, 1996; Hayward et al., 2004). Although other types of haptic feedback devices exist (e.g. tension-based and vibrotactile), these devices represent the bulk of what is presently sold and used.

Data Gloves

Immersion Corporation, who offer "hand-centric hardware and software solutions for animating hand movements and manipulating graphical objects with physical hands" (http://www.immersion.com/), stands out as a leader in the development of data gloves. To summarize the technology briefly, they employ resistive bend-sensing technology to accurately transform hand and finger motions into real-time joint-angle data (up to 22 joint-angle measurements) as the position and orientation of the user's hand and fingers are tracked in the virtual 3-D environment. Their product line includes the CyberGrasp™, a lightweight, force-reflecting exoskeleton that fits over their CyberGlove® and adds resistive force feedback to each finger (shown in Figure 2).

Figure 2. Immersion Technologies' CyberGrasp™ exoskeleton over their CyberGlove®.

Point-Probes

Occupying much the second class of haptic devices are tools developed by SensAble Technologies, Inc. Their point-probe devices are effectively small, desk-grounded robot-like arms that permit simulation of contact with virtual objects via a pen-like stylus (see Figure 3). These devices are capable of tracking the x, y, and z coordinates, as well as the pitch, roll, and yaw of the virtual point-probe as the user moves it about a 3D workspace. Actuators (motors within the device) communicate preprogrammed forces back to the user's fingertips as it detects collisions with the virtual objects rendered, simulating the sense of touch.

Figure 3. The PHANToM® Omni ™ desktop device from SensAble Technologies, Inc.

HAP TIC INFORMATION PROCESSING

Hands-on Learning?

The idea of a hands-on, minds-on curriculum is not new. An emphasis on actively involving students in learning has influenced American schools throughout its history. Early advocates, such as John Dewey, suggested that this mode of instruction was indispensable with statements such as: "The map does not take the place of the actual journey. The logically formulated material of a science is no substitute for the having of individual experiences. The mathematical formula for a falling body does not take the place of personal contact and immediate individual experience with the falling thing." (Dewey, 1902, p. 20).

One can reasonably argue that the haptic augmentation of Serious Games, ones in which the students are active participants, represent an exciting innovation in the design of computer-based teaching/learning technologies. In fact, theoretical claims abound (e.g. McMurray, 1921; Piaget, 1954; Fitts & Posner, 1967; Wadsworth, 1989; Reiner, 1999; Williams, et al., 2003). Some suggest that the addition of haptics affords student users the opportunity to become more fully immersed in this meaning-making process, leading to more connected and more robust understandings. Others contend that haptic feedback conjures up experiential or embodied knowledge that would otherwise lie untapped in the recesses of our long term memory. But despite a voluminous literature base from the fields of developmental and cognitive psychology regarding underlying principles and processes of the haptic perception and cognition, very little is known about the true educational impact of haptic technology (Minogue & Jones, 2006).

Visual-Haptic Perception

What we do know is that haptics is superior to vision in the perception of *material properties* such as texture (i.e. roughness/smoothness, hardness/softness, wetness/dryness, stickiness, and slipperiness) and microspatial properties of pattern, compliance, elasticity, and viscosity (Lederman, 1983; Zangaladze et al., 1999). Conversely, it has been demonstrated in numerous studies that vision dominates in the perception of *geometric properties* such as size and shape (Heller, 1982; Sathian et al., 1997; Verry, 1998).

There is also mounting neurological evidence suggesting that visual and haptic object representations are so similar that they might be shared. For example, researchers have used functional magnetic resonance (fMRI) imaging to show that the neural substrate underlying both visual and haptic object recognition lies within the occipital cortex associated with visual processing (e.g. Damasio, 1989; Sathian et al., 1997; Deibert et al., 1999; Zangaladze et al., 1999; Amedi et al., 2001; Ernst & Banks, 2004; Drewing & Ernst, 2006). It should be noted that a comprehensive discussion of the research base regarding visual-haptic-interactions lies well beyond the scope of this chapter.

Our current understandings of haptic information processing, as it pertains to teaching with serious games, are somewhat restricted due to the simple fact that much of the fundamental research regarding haptic perception (e.g. Lederman & Klatzky, 1987; Lederman & Klatzky, 1990; Lederman, Summers, & Klatzky, 1996; Klatzky & Lederman, 1999) was conducted with subjects in controlled settings deprived of vision. This is a far different scenario than the one created by adding haptics to a Serious Gaming environment; situations in which players receive bi-modal feedback and can take advantage of both visual and haptic information as they progress through virtual worlds.

Several crucial core questions remain unanswered: Does the unique bi-directional exchange of information between a user and a haptic device somehow enhance the learning experience? What type of haptic information do individuals find salient and choose to attend to? How is this haptic information organized and integrated by the learner? Work in this arena is still in its infancy and there exists a critical need for more systematic investigations of how students perceive, process, store, and make use of haptic information.

HAPTICALLY AUGMENTED SERIOUS GAMES

Fertile Ground

In 2006, retail sales of video games (which include portable and console hardware, software, PC games, and accessories) generated revenues of close to $13.5 billion in the United States alone. According to The NPD Group, Inc. (www.npd.com), a leading marketing information provider, this represents an 18% increase over the previous year, and a 15% increase over the record earnings achieved in 2002. Given these staggering numbers, it is not surprising that there has been a blossoming interest in expanding this market into education. In recent years the creation of computer-based games for use in training and teaching scenarios has taken off. Whether called *Serious Games* or *educational games*, these instructional computer games are characterized by varying degrees of fantasy, sensory stimuli, challenge, mystery, and control. Player interactions with real world systems within a virtual world are governed by rules and goals. These educational games commonly require the use of logic, memory, problem solving and critical thinking skills, as well as visualization and discovery.

No doubt, currently available Serious Games are able to provide a level of engagement that has been linked to enhanced motivation and increased student interest in subject matter (e.g. Barab et al., 2001, 2005; Garris, et al., 2002; Prensky, 2001; Squire, 2002; Taradi, 2005). One of the key strengths of serious games is that they can allow students to observe, explore, recreate, manipulate variables, and receive immediate feedback about objects and events that would be too time-consuming, costly, and/or dangerous to experience first hand during traditional school science lessons (Winn, 2002).

Plotting a Course

The true pedagogical power of Serious Games may not be realized until we begin to augment these games with haptic feedback. The game players' sense of *presence*, a common measure of an immersive experience, will almost certainly be heightened with the addition of touch. Incorporating haptic technology is a logical and exciting next step in the development of these Serious Games. It represents a means by which we can extend student users' ability to interact in a variety of technology-enhanced learning environments.

Imagine the creation of a Serious Game that teaches middle school students about energy transformations and mechanical motion be infusing these science concepts into a digital game-based learning environment. Here students are challenged to advance an ancient civilization through the design, building, and testing and refining of machines (e.g. inclined plane, levers, pulley systems ...). Now imagine that through haptic augmentation students could "feel" the effort forces, frictional forces, mechanical advantage, and efficiency associated with their designs. Envision the creation of a serious game that challenges shipwrecked students to devise a way to escape a deserted island by building a seaworthy vessel while learning about buoyancy and basic engineering concepts. Now envision students being able to not only see but also "feel" the forces associated with sinking and floating such as gravity pushing down, buoyant forces pushing up, surface tension, as well as the mass of displaced water.

Perhaps surprisingly, these above described scenarios are not wild-eyed fantasies; rather they are quickly becoming reality. Recently, *Novint Technologies, Inc.* (http://www.novint.com/) unveiled its *Falcon*. This point-probe haptic device provides high fidelity 3-DOF force feedback as it track x, y, and z coordinates in a computer generated virtual environment (Figure 4).

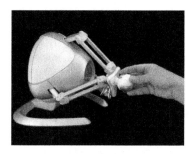

Figure 4. The Falcon by Novint Technologies Inc.

Available in the summer 2007, the *Falcon* retails for under $100 in mass market quantities. Even more encouraging is the fact that *Novint Technologies* has developed a 3D touch Application Programming Interface (API) and *Half Life® 2* device drivers for modding the *Valve Corporation's Source™* engine (http://www.valvesoftware.com). This 3D game engine, the same used to build and power the popular *Half-Life 2* game, is available for license by third party developers and it features a high degree of modularity and flexibility, as well as a powerful and efficient physics system.

Cautious Optimism

The research community should approach the creation and deployment of haptically augmented Serious Games with tempered enthusiasm. That is, we need to recognize ineffectiveness of incorporating this type of technology haphazardly or in isolation (Bayraktar, 2002; Hsu & Thomas, 2002). The implementation guidelines put forth by Smetana and Bell (2006) appear to be timely and astute. It is suggested that innovative technologies, such as serious games and haptics, should supplement and enhance (not replace) other modes of instruction such as hands-on labs and activities currently included in many inquiry-based educational programs.

Perhaps even more importantly, there is a critical need for research that systematically links the basic research on haptic cognition with the applied research on haptics as an intervention for change; work that seeks to apply the knowledge creation of basic research to achieve beneficial effects in real-world classrooms (Minogue & Jones, 2006). I speculate that the combined impact of continued advances in haptic technology and a more complete understanding of haptic information processing will lead to the prudent evolution of haptically rich serious games.

REFERENCES

Amedi, A., Malach, R., Hendler, T., Peled, S., & Zohary, E. (2001). Visuo-hap tic object-related activation in the ventral visual pathway. *Nature Neuroscience, 4*, 324-30.

Barab, S., Thomas, M., Dodge, T., Carteaux, R., & Tuzun, H. (2005). Making learning fun: Quest Atlantis, a game without guns. *Educational Technology Research and Development, 53*, 86–107.

Barab, S. A., Hay, K. E., Barnett, M. G., & Squire, K. (2001). Constructing virtual worlds: Tracing the historical development of learner practices/understandings. *Cognition and Instruction, 19*(1), 47–94.

Bayraktar, S. (2002). A meta-analysis of the effectiveness of computer-assisted instruction in science education. *Journal of Research on Technology in Education, 34*(2), 173-188.

Burdea, G. C. (1996). *Force and touch feedback for virtual reality.* New York: John Wiley.

Damasio, A.R. (1989). The brain binds entities and events by multiregional activation from convergence zones. *Neural Computation, 1*, 123-132.

Deibert, E., Kraut, M., Kremen, S., & Hart, J.J. (1999). Neural pathways in tactile object recognition. *Neurology, 52*, 1413-1417.

Dewey, J. (1902). *The child and the curriculum.* Chicago: University of Chicago Press.

Drewing, K. & Ernst, M.O. (2006). Integration of force and position cues for shape perception through active touch. *Brain Research, 1078*(1), 92-100.

Ernst, M.O. & Banks, M.S. (2004). Humans integrate visual and haptic information in a statistically optimal fashion. *Nature, 415*(6870), 429-433.

Fitts, P. & Posner, M. (1967). *Human performance.* Belmont, CA: Brooks/Cole.

Garris, R., Ahlers, R., & Driskell, J.E. (2002). Games, motivation, and learning: A research and practice model. *Simulation & Gaming, 33*(4), 441-467.

Goertz, R. C. (1952). Fundamentals of general purpose remote manipulators. *Nucleonics, 10*, 36-42.

Goertz, R. C. (1964). Manipulator systems development at ANL. Proc. 12th Conference on Remote System Technology.

Hatwell, Y., Streri, A. & Gentaz, E. (2003). *Touching for knowing.* Amsterdam/Philadelphia: John Benjamins Publishing Company.

Hayward, V., Oliver, R. A., Cruz-Hernandez, M., Grant, D., & Robles-De-La-Torre, G. (2004). Haptic interfaces and devices. *Sensor Review, 24*, 16–29.

Heller, M.A. (1982). Visual and tactual texture perception: Intersensory cooperation. *Perception and Psychophysics, 31*, 339-344.

Hsu, Y. & Thomas, R. (2002). The impacts of a web-aided instructional simulation on science learning. *International Journal of Science Education, 24*(9), 955-979.

Immersion Corporation, Inc., http://www.immersion.com/

Jacobson, R. D., Kitchen, R., & Golledge, R. (2002). Multimodal virtual reality for presenting geographic information. In P. Fisher & D. Unwin (Eds.), *Virtual reality in geography* (pp. 382-401). New York, NY: Taylor & Francis, Inc.

Katz, D. (1989). *The world of touch* (L. Krueger, Trans.). Hillsdale, NJ: Erlbaum. (Original work published 1925)

Klatzky, R. L. & Lederman, S. J. (1999). The haptic glance: A route to rapid object identification and manipulation. In D. Gopher & A. Koriat (eds.), *Attention and Performance XVII: Cognitive regulation of performance: Interaction of theory and application* (pp. 165-196). Mahwah, NJ: Erlbaum.

Lederman, S. (1983). Tactile roughness perception: Spatial and temporal determinants. *Canadian Journal of Psychology, 37*, 498-511.

Lederman, S.J., & Klatzky, R.L., (1987). Hand movements: A window into haptic object recognition. *Cognitive Psychology, 19*, 342-368.

Lederman, S. J., & Klatzky, R. L. (1990). Haptic classification of common objects: Knowledge driven exploration. *Cognitive Psychology, 22*, 421-459.

Lederman, W., Summers, C., & Klatzky, R. (1996). Cognitive salience of haptic object properties: Role of modality-encoding bias. *Perception, 25*, 983-998.

McLaughlin, M., Hespanha, J., & Sukhatme, G. (2002). *Touch in virtual environments: Haptics and the design of interactive systems.* Upper Saddle River, NJ: Prentice Hall.

McMurray, C. A. (1921). *Teaching by projects: A basis for purposeful study.* New York: Macmillan.

Minogue, J. & Jones, M.G. (2006). Haptics in education: Exploring an untapped sensory modality. *Review of Educational Research, 76*(3), 317-348.

The NPD Group, Inc., http://www.npd.com/

Novint Technologies, http://www.novint.com/

Piaget, J. (1954). *The construction of reality in the child.* New York: Basic Books.

Prensky, M. (2001). *Digital game-based learning.* New York: McGraw-Hill

Reiner, M. (1999). Conceptual construction of fields through tactile interface. *Interactive Learning Environments, 7*, 31-55.

Revesz, G. (1950). *The psychology and art of the blind.* London: Longmans Green.

Robles-De-La-Torre, G. (2006) The importance of the sense of touch in virtual and real environments. *IEEE Multimedia*, Special issue on Haptic User Interfaces for Multimedia Systems, *13*(3), 24-30.

Sathian, K., Zangaladze, A., Hoffman, J., & Grafton, S. (1997). Feeling with the mind's eye. *Neuroreport, 8*, 3877–3881.

SensAble Technologies, Inc., http://www.sensable.com/

Smetana, L.K., & Bell, R.L. (2006). Simulating science. *School Science and Mathematics, 106*, 267-271.

Squire, K. (2002). Cultural framing of computer/video games. *International Journal of Computer Game Research, 2*(1).

Taradi, S. K., Taradi, M., Radic, K., & Pokrajac, N. (2005). Blending problem-based learning with Web technology positively impacts student learning outcomes in acid-base physiology. *Journal of Advanced Pysiological Education, 29*, 35-39.

Valve Corporation, http://www.valvesoftware.com/about.html

Verry, R. (1998). Don't take touch for granted: An interview with Susan Lederman. *Teaching Psychology, 25*, 64-67.

Wadsworth, B. (1989). *Piaget's theory of cognitive and affective development.* New York: Longman.

Williams, R.L., Chen, M., & Seaton, J.M. (2003). Haptics-augmented simple-machine educational tools. *Journal of Science Education and Technology, 12*, 1-12

Winn, W. (2002). Current Trends in Educational Technology Research: The Study of Learning Environments. *Educational Psychology Review, 14*(3), 331-351.

Zangaladze, A., Epstein C.M., Grafton, S.T., & Sathian, K. (1999). Involvement of visual cortex in tactile discrimination of orientation. *Nature, 401*, 587-90.

James Minogue
Department of Elementary Education,
North Carolina State University

CPSIA information can be obtained at www.ICGtesting.com
Printed in the USA
BVOW11s1112130116

432750BV00035B/209/P

9 789087 903794